Dear Target Shopper,

First of all, turn around. I am probably standing right behind you. Not because I am following you. Because I am also shopping at Target. Also, well, maybe I *am* following you. So what? I wasn't sure if you were someone I went to high school with. And how else am I supposed to find out?

Anyway, I love Target. I have loved it since I was a little girl. I loved it before it was even cool to call it "Tar-Zhay." And I want to tell you that I have never, ever called it "Tar-Zhay." It is not where you go to "zhay" your stuff. It is where you go to "get" your stuff. And Target is where we are both shopping, right now.

When I was growing up in St. Louis, my mom used to take me to Target on Saturday mornings. We would drop off my little sister, Carrie, at her gymnastics class in Kirkwood, pump up KLOU 103 (the oldies station), and floor it to this dream store for household supplies, sweaters and shoes, and even the occasional electronic good. Target gives me a sense of security that I get nowhere else in this world. I feel safe, and I feel happy. And I do feel bad that I never attended a single one of Carrie's gymnastics meets.

Thank you for pausing by the book section. And thank you even more for picking up my book. This book is all about a young dork becoming an older dork. And that dork is me. I hope that these stories of me being a dork entertain you. I hope they make you laugh. Because, truly, that is all I want to do here. I want you to be able to take a break, relax, and smile. The world is rough right now. This book should be a vacation from that.

Speaking of vacations—I won't keep you from your Target vacation any longer. Enjoy the cooling breezes and serene clearance sections this store has to offer us!!! And I'm sorry for mistaking you—we didn't go to high school together. But if you don't hurry, I am going to get to the athleisure section before you.

xo Ellie

My Squirrel Days

ELLIE KEMPER

SCRIBNER
New York London Toronto Sydney New Delhi

Scribner
An Imprint of Simon & Schuster, Inc.
1230 Avenue of the Americas
New York, NY 10020

An earlier version of "Hysteric" ran on *McSweeney's Internet Tendency*.
Some of the materials in this book originally appeared in *The New York Times*
and is reprinted by permission.

Certain names have been changed.

This Scribner hardcover edition October 2018

Interior design by Erich Hobbing

Manufactured in the United States of America

1 3 5 7 9 10 8 6 4 2

Library of Congress Cataloging-in-Publication Data is available.

ISBN 978-1-9821-1333-9

Photograph credits: page 3 © Kris Carr; page 40 by Steve Granitz/WireImage;
pages 94, 121, 138, 215, and 230 courtesy of the author

For Mom and Dad

Loving, smart, and just so funny

Contents

CONTENTS

My Squirrel Days

Author

There comes a time in every sitcom actress's life when she is faced with the prospect of writing a book. When my number was up, I told myself that I would not blink. I would fulfill my duty as an upbeat actress under contract on a television series and serve my country in the only way I knew how. I would cull from my life the very greatest and most memorable of anecdotes, I would draw on formative lessons learned both early on and also not too long ago, I would paint for the reader a portrait of the girl, the teenager, the *woman* I am today, and I would not falter. I would write a book.

And so, Reader, I got to work.

First, I started dressing like an Author: black turtlenecks and dark denim jeans. Then, I started sipping like an Author: double shots of espresso with no Hershey's syrup to cushion the blow. Finally, I started talking like an Author: "That reminds me of my book," I would begin most sentences. I noticed people stopped talking to me as much.

But onward I marched.

I reread all the classics: *Pride and Prejudice*, *The Catcher in the Rye*, *What to Expect When You're Expecting*. I scribbled in journals and I sighed with meaning. All shaving came to an immediate and powerful halt. Did I stumble in my journey? Of course I did. *Nothing ventured, nothing gained*, I would remind myself as I boldly considered mixing two flavors of Ben and Jerry's that I had never tasted together before. *Also, you should try writing the first paragraph of your book*, I would add, after I had declared my new frozen dairy creation a success.

Heroes are not born; they are made. Nonetheless, being an Author is exhausting. I would struggle to fall asleep at night, tossing and turning in the way that only a tortured artist can. "Is this how Chaucer felt?!" I cried out to the big black darkness. "You are being so loud!" hushed my now-awake husband. I envied his innocence. You see, Reader, I knew that I had *some* great wisdom to offer you, but I worried that I did not have *enough* great wisdom to give to you. And this worry very nearly destroyed me.

I began losing interest in food.[1] I found little joy in the things I used to love.[2] I had to wonder: is all of this Life really worth it?[3]

And then, one Sunday afternoon, alone in my closet, sifting through a bunch of broken memories and Spanx so stretched out they were no longer useful, I came across my very first headshot:

1 Absolutely untrue.

2 *The Marvelous Mrs. Maisel*, but that is only because I watched the pilot in October, and then had to wait a full two months for the second episode! By then I was so frustrated that I didn't even care anymore!

3 Referring to the cereal. Went waaay overboard at a "buy one get one half off" sale at Fairway that week.

AUTHOR

I stared at the woman in this photo. "*I know you*," I whispered. "Oh, wait. You're me." For a second, I had thought it was an old picture of Prince Harry. Anyway, there I was. At the time of that headshot, I was twenty-three years old, but I look both fourteen and eighty-seven. The photo was taken by Kris Carr, a beautiful vegan who wore tank tops in winter and cooked us black beans and sautéed kale for lunch. Besides my pale, remarkably round face, every inch of my skin is covered in this portrait. I am wearing a brown corduroy jacket from the Gap and a beige turtleneck that threatens to swallow me whole. My left forearm is placed casually on my right knee, suggesting that I am a strong woman with definite opinions but also that I am able to kick back and relax like an easygoing cowboy. Very little attention was paid to hair or makeup that day, but my mischievous smile assures you that I am crushing life and also that I might just have a secret or two tucked up that corduroy sleeve.

I looked at that girl and I missed her. She was full of light, of hope, and her cheeks looked like they were storing nuts. Had this girl moved on to learn anything of substance over the next fifteen years? Nah. But she did remind me of the power in pretending. She also reminded me that the Gap seems to have great sales just about every other day (at least online).

The Ellie in that headshot was not only a dead ringer for British royalty, but she was also pretending to be confident at a time in her life when, frankly, she felt a little bit lost. *Wait a minute*, I realized a few hours later over an exciting new mix of The Tonight Dough with Peanut Buttah Cookie Core: *I do have enough wisdom to share!* Corduroy Ellie may have been smiling bravely, but there was a considerable amount of doubt and fear hiding behind that smile. *And yet Corduroy Ellie did not let the doubt and fear win.*

As a reasonably talented person who is also part fraud, I cannot praise highly enough the virtues of enthusiasm and tenacity as substitutes for finely honed skills or intensive training. And in this book, Reader, I will tell you about the numerous times that I have made up in pluck what I have lacked in natural ability. I will reveal tidbits from my past, and I will feed you morsels from the present. Some stories might seem implausible, some anecdotes farfetched. And I am here to tell you that this is because I have made them up. What do you want from me? I have an energetic toddler and my memory is fuzzy.

Here are some of the tales I have to share:

- My exhilarating rise—though some have described it as more of a "flatline"—through NCAA Division I College Field Hockey. A very thin woman with a bionic knee plays a prominent role.
- A ruthless exposé of my personal encounters with some of the splashiest personalities in Hollywood. Cameos include Pulitzer Prize–winning historian Doris Kearns Goodwin and the late Pope John Paul II.
- Filming the movie *Bridesmaids* while simultaneously serving as a bridesmaid in real life. Art and life grew inextricable, and I slowly began to lose my mind.
- My platonic yet breathless pursuit of a turquoise-pants-loving second-grade student teacher named Ms. Romanoff—and how her Russian heritage would ultimately teach me that even though Russia might have interfered with our 2016 election, it doesn't mean that the entire country is bad.
- Why being a mom is hard, but trying to remain rational while hungry is even harder.

In closing, I would like to share some writing advice I once received from an old graduate school professor:[4] Write like your parents are dead. Free yourself from any harnesses or constraints that are keeping you from telling your truth. And do not worry about whether you are doing the right thing or the wrong thing. *Just be honest.*

Well, I don't write like my parents are dead. I write like they are alive, thriving, and peering over my shoulder. I'm not sure that's a bad thing. Aren't parents supposed to be your moral

4 Found by googling "best way to write a book is what?"

guides? Not only do I not want to embarrass my mom or my dad, but I happen to think they have pretty good judgment. Also, I need them on my good side if I want them to keep giving fun grandparent gifts to my son. As far as being honest, I already told you that a lot of the details and dialogue here are made up.

I have learned that an Author must write what She knows. And I, for one, happen to know a lot about snacks. In fact, this book is not so much a tribute to brave women everywhere as it is a record of my favorite ice cream brands. So you see, I wrote what I knew, and I know what I wrote. I hope that you enjoy.

Best,
Ellie Kemper

Hero

Waldo, a double-pint-sized stuffed walrus, was given to me on my eighth birthday by the most beautiful woman in the world, a student teacher at Conway School in St. Louis named Ms. Romanoff. He was accompanied by three beanbag frogs—Wilbur, Paisley, and Caplis—but it is Waldo with whom I have slept every night since. The frogs were nice, but they leaked sand and smelled like yeast. Waldo smells like Bounce and wears a small white sailor's cap that suggests he is not opposed to a good time.

Ms. Romanoff captivated me from the first day of second grade—and I wasn't the only one to fall under her spell. As Mrs. Goode, our primary teacher, introduced Ms. Romanoff to us, a hush fell over the class. This princess-like, curly-haired brunette got up quietly from her desk in the back and walked past me, leaving me in a haze of some sort of otherworldly scent—was it Windsong? Electric Youth? (those were the only two perfumes I knew)—before reaching the chalkboard at the front of the room. Her voice was soft, and her eyes were large. She told us that she was twenty-five years old, that her parents had come to St. Louis from Russia, and that her favorite holiday was Hanukkah. I couldn't take my eyes off her outfit: bright pastel blue pants with white suspenders and a bright pastel blue blazer to match. I had never seen anyone so well dressed. I hung on every word that came out of her mouth; her voice sounded how my Eggo syrup tasted. I looked around at the other kids in the class; Julie Ryan looked hypnotized, and Connor Blake was picking his nose. Allison Edwards tapped me on the shoulder. "Isn't Russia our enemy?" she whispered, looking worried. "It's fine," I told her. "Stop talking when she's talking!" I added. The truth is, I was worried, too. Wasn't Hanukkah Jewish? I couldn't get my own Sunday school teacher's lessons out of my head. Had the Jewish people actually been mad at Jesus? Sister Agnes knew everything about the Bible, but she was also very old; I hoped this dear nun was just confused. The beautiful woman before me—a kind Russian daughter who went nuts for Hanukkah—couldn't possibly come from a place of anger. I turned back to face Ms. Romanoff and gave her my most radiant smile. *Move over, Sister Agnes*, I thought to myself. *There's a new teacher in town.* I decided right then and there that Ms. Romanoff would be my best friend.

Frankly, I needed one. I was hardly the first seven-year-old to observe that second grade, in no uncertain terms, is a shit show. Gone were the naps of kindergarten and the double recesses of first grade. As much as we all liked to think that sleeping during the day was just for babies, the truth was we needed those naps. Going outside just once in the afternoon was hard. Staying inside and working all morning made us feel like prisoners, or worse: businessmen. My mom no longer packed a lunch for me if I didn't like what was on the school lunch menu, so if I wanted other food, *I had to pack it myself.* An outsider might think that was freeing, but in fact, I still had to show my mom the lunch bag before I left for school: one sandwich, one piece of fruit, and one bag of chips or dessert. Try opening up that brown sack next to Lindsay Howard and her Punky Brewster lunchbox overflowing with Bugles and Twix, and then try to feel one ounce of dignity.

I would sometimes sigh as we finished another chapter of *The Boxcar Children*. "I'll tell you one thing," I'd mutter to Jerry Glen. "Some days, living in a rusty boxcar seems a lot easier than a day in this class." It wasn't that I was jealous of the children in the boxcar, exactly, but at least they didn't have to scan the *St. Louis Post-Dispatch* every Tuesday morning for an interesting current-events article and clip it out to read in front of the entire class. Jerry was a nice guy who never understood the "your epidermis is showing" joke but never got sick of hearing it. "You're nasty, Ellie!" he would shout. I guess nobody ever told Jerry your epidermis is just your skin.

Every day after recess, we would return to the classroom and write in our journals. These journals, we had been told, were different from personal diaries, because spelling and grammar mattered. While we were not officially graded on our entries, Ms. Romanoff would read them at the end of the twenty-minute writing session, going around the room and writing responses to nearly every student. As I do the math now, the whole thing must have taken close to an hour; one-sixth of every second-grade school day was devoted to journaling. Is it any wonder, then, that I do not know the chronological order of my country's presidents?

I craved Ms. Romanoff's comments like oxygen. Clean, confident, and elegant, her handwriting was as inspiring as the words themselves. *I'm going to write like that when I grow up*, I would think to myself. *I am going to wear bright blue pants and have double pierced ears and handwriting like Ms. Romanoff.* I would look at my own childish scrawl next to the flowing script of this fully formed woman and blush. I had a long way to go.

In Mrs. Goode's class, alliances were shifting constantly. Someone who was your friend on Tuesday morning might very well be your worst enemy by Wednesday afternoon. Ms. Romanoff understood this. *I just don't know what I ever did to Ruth Weber*, I wrote one day after recess. *I thought we were friends, but today, I asked if she wanted to split my Ladue Mini Burger with me, and she left the table*. Ladue was the name of my school district, and Mini Burger Day was the day they served small, gray hamburgers. I couldn't understand why Ruth had walked away from me with no explanation.

Maybe Ruth doesn't like hamburgers, Ms. Romanoff wrote back, her penmanship immaculate as the driven snow. That was all that she wrote that day, but every word was a golden truth. At the end of the school day, in the bus line, I went up to Ruth. "Hey," I said softly. "Are you mad at me? Or do you just not like hamburgers?" Ruth laughed. "I don't like *those* hamburgers. They're hard." We both smiled, and I probably gave her a high five. Overwhelmed by the day's events, I accidentally got on the wrong bus that afternoon, but I didn't care. At the end of Bus 5's route, Miss Abigail brought me back to the school. When my mom picked me up with my older brother, John, sitting in the front, I smiled at them as I slipped into the backseat. "It's good to have friends," I whispered, clutching both their hands. "But you don't have any," John observed, shoving my hand away.

Eve Batey was a pistol, a real firecracker of a girl. Once, I showed up to school wearing the exact same outfit as her: green leggings and a white top with green trim and a print of yellow Scottie dogs. Eve told me that if I didn't change my shirt, she would punch my guts out. I told her, desperately, that I didn't have another shirt with me. Eve considered this and then changed her mind. "I guess it's okay for today," she told me. "But if you ever wear that shirt again, I'll punch your guts out." Eve Batey could be explosive, but she was not unreasonable.

I really want to teach Eve to fight with words, and not fists, I wrote thoughtfully one afternoon. *Violence isn't the answer.* Writing in my journal was a tightrope walk. I knew that Ms. Romanoff would be reading my entry, but I had to write as though I were completely unaware of this. In the words of a needlepoint pillow my step-grandmother once had, I had to dance like no one was watching—but I still had to look good (only that first part was on the pillow). Candid thoughts had to be tweaked slightly; I couldn't let Ms. Romanoff see the dark underside of Ellie just yet. I needed, first and foremost, to gain her respect.

You should always tell a teacher if anyone is ever fighting with fists, Ms. Romanoff wrote back. *A teacher can take care of the situation better than a student*. I wasn't sure what to do with this. Was she reprimanding me? I felt embarrassed. The school day ended before I had a chance to clear things up with her, so the next morning I went straight to her desk, not even stopping by Cubby Corner first to put away my backpack. "Ms. Romanoff," I said. "I just wanted to let you know that I know the teacher is always in charge. That's why they are the teacher." Ms. Romanoff smiled at me, and nodded. I began to walk away, not sure whether I had made things better or much, much worse. "Ellie!" Ms. Romanoff called out. I turned back around. "What a great headband that is! It goes beautifully with your red hair." I touched my pink headband with the oversized magenta bow and grinned. I was back.

As the year went on, my journal entries evolved. I gradually became the hero of every story. If someone had been a victim, I was the one who came to his rescue. If a friend and I were in a fight, I was the one who took the high road. *Mrs. Stafford asked if anyone would be willing to take the flies home from Idea Lab*, I wrote one February morning. We had been growing larvae in this after-school program, and now that the pupae had developed into the flies they were always meant to become, our studies were complete. *Nobody raised their hand. But if we let the flies out into the world, they will be lost.* I took a deep breath and began a fresh paragraph. *So I will take them home.*

Ms. Romanoff was busy reading Thomas Whipp's journal, and I waited. As she approached my desk pod, I decided I would be able to see her reaction better from a distance. I got up, muttering something about sharpening my pencil, and walked backward toward Book Barn, keeping my eyes on Ms. Romanoff the whole time. Imagine my excitement when I saw the smile dance on her lips as she read my entry. She even shook her head, most likely in awe, as she began her written response. *It will be nice to have some pets. I hope that your mom likes the flies.* Ms. Romanoff knew that we didn't have any pets, and that John really wanted a dog. *I am sure Mrs. Stafford appreciates it, too.* When I returned to Desk Pod 3 and read those words, I felt like jumping up and down.

Later that evening, after dinner, my dad would go downstairs to find that there was a hole in the screen of the Idea Lab Fly Box and the flies were now swarming the basement. "The flies are on the loose!" he shouted. We opened the basement doors and shooed them all outside, but I didn't tell Ms. Romanoff that part.

I could never tell Ms. Romanoff that part.

Everyone says that Mrs. Klein wears a wig, I wrote in early March. *Oliver Tates says he is going to try and knock it off her during dodgeball.* Rumor had it that our PE teacher was not naturally endowed with an auburn bob; apparently, she had been bald ever since she began teaching at the school in the 1960s. Oliver Tates knew this, he claimed, because his older sister had seen her adjusting her wig in the bathroom more than a decade earlier.

I told Oliver that he should leave Mrs. Klein alone. I told him that sometimes people wear wigs because they are embarrassed about their natural hair. In fact, I had never told Oliver anything of the sort. At the lunch table earlier that day, I had nodded and giggled along with everyone else, scared that if I didn't, people might think that I, too, wore an auburn wig. Ms. Romanoff wrote back that teachers are just people, and she agreed with me that Oliver should not try to knock the wig off Mrs. Klein's head. My heart soared. Not only did Ms. Romanoff approve of my tough words to Oliver (tough words that had never been said at all), but in her own indirect way, she was trying to tell me that she, a teacher, was also a person—no different from me. The impeccable blue ink held special meaning for me that day.

That spring, I played the lead in our grade's production of *Get Hoppin'*. As Bunny Sue, I was the rebellious rabbit who refused to learn how to hop. I lashed out at my siblings, pulling their ears and sticking out my tongue at them. Behind the scenes, however, I worked hard to reassure my castmates that I was not a diva in real life. There was no task too mundane for me to complete; with every action, I sought to convince my peers that I was just like them. *Victor Pine needed help with his tail today*, I wrote during rehearsal week. *I told him that I could pin it on him, but I didn't want to make him uncomfortable by accidentally touching his bumper*. Ms. Romanoff agreed that Victor should be in charge of pinning his own tail on his own rear end, but that it was always good to think of other people. I shuddered. Did Ms. Romanoff think I had actually wanted to touch Victor Pine's bumper? The next day, I clarified that I had planned to help pin Victor's tail on his costume *before* he changed into it; the costume, a one-piece footed fleece pajama suit, had been lying on the table, far away from Victor's bumper. Ms. Romanoff remarked that she heard I was a wonderful Bunny Sue and that she couldn't wait for the performance that Thursday. My feet hardly touched the ground for the rest of the day. Ms. Romanoff thought I was a star.

It was not uncommon for girls in the class to invite Ms. Romanoff to their birthday parties. It seemed to me that even our own mothers and fathers could not resist the charms of this Russian-American lady. I guess they saw in Ms. Romanoff the same things that we all saw: a warm woman with a gracious smile and a ton of bright blue pants. When Ms. Romanoff attended my own eighth birthday party in May, she wore teal jeans with a slightly lighter teal cardigan. Her white Keds matched her white cotton T-shirt, and her ears sported four individual crescent moon posts. Ms. Romanoff stayed on after the other girls had left and ate dinner with my family. After homemade chocolate cake with mocha icing, we moved to the den to open presents, and Ms. Romanoff bestowed upon me one awesome gift after another. She gave me a translucent wand with water and glitter inside. She gave me a book of astrology and a black mask covered in gold stars. She gave me several charcoal-colored stones and handwritten instructions to blow on them while making a wish. I have a picture of me from that night, wearing the black mask, wielding the wand, and holding up the book as the rest of my family looks on, confused. *What in the fuck is going on there?* my husband once asked me. The final installment of gifts from Ms. Romanoff, the prized float in that parade of enchantment, was the box that held Wilbur, Paisley, Caplis—and Waldo. While these guys didn't fit in with the mystical theme, that was okay. Waldo was unequivocally adorable, and I knew even then that astrology might come and go, but a stuffed walrus would always stay true.

The 1987–1988 school year would end on June 7, and Ms. Romanoff would not be returning the following year. I still am not sure where she went after Mrs. Goode's class. I don't even remember saying good-bye. Years later, when I was in high school, I received a letter from her. She was married now, she had moved to Germany, and she had a little baby girl. She enclosed a photo of her with her darling daughter, and I hardly recognized Ms. Romanoff. Her hair was now straight, and she wasn't wearing any makeup. I guess she had always been wearing makeup when she was my teacher; I had never noticed. I couldn't believe how, in a single photo, Ms. Romanoff had gone from untouchable angel to mere mortal. *Is this what happens to all student teachers?* I had to wonder.

I turned to Waldo, and I showed him the letter. "This is your grandmother," I breathed. I wasn't sure if, technically, that's what Ms. Romanoff was to Waldo, but I also knew that Waldo was too laid-back to care about such semantics. To say that Waldo helped me see the lighter side of life would be an understatement. My walrus was a calm, mellow, unflappable guy who certainly cared about the world and his own place in it—but he also knew that sometimes you just had to throw up your hands and laugh. After all, how much control do we really have? Waldo possessed a wisdom beyond his years, and since his birth in my childhood den, he had brought me more joy and more comfort than any other single object in my twin bed's pillow arrangement.

When it came time for college, Waldo was the lone stuffed animal from my collection to make the trek with me. I had considered taking my pink bunny (Bunny), or even Caplis—Wilbur and Paisley were leaking at an alarming rate by that point, and such a treacherous journey was out of the question—but in the end, I knew that Waldo was the only stuffie strong enough to provide the support I would so desperately need in this new stage of my life. I turned out to be right. Waldo kept me grounded in the whirlwind of classes, parties, and all-you-can-eat dining-hall fro-yo; he comforted me in the face of heartbreak. Waldo knew this was my first time living away from home, and he saw that I was scared. "I know it doesn't smell as good here," I would whisper to him before going to sleep. "But I promise I am going to change my sheets next week." In fact, I would go on to wash my sheets only two times my freshman year, and one of those times was when I took them home to St. Louis for Thanksgiving. Waldo endured all with a smile and—I think I saw once?—a tip of his sailor's cap. He remained my constant companion through graduation and beyond.

In 2012, several months before my own wedding, my younger sister, Carrie, threw me a bachelorette party in Las Vegas. I had the time of my life, but when I returned home to Los Angeles that Sunday night, I was alarmed to find that Waldo was missing from my suitcase. I called the Wynn Hotel in a panic to see if anyone had reported a misplaced stuffed walrus. I was asked to describe the walrus. I thought about it for a moment. "He's a small wisp of a thing with a twinkle in his eye," I said softly. The woman on the phone asked me to speak up because she couldn't hear me. I cleared my throat. "He is a stuffed walrus in the shape of a small walrus," I said. But the young woman told me that no one had seen Waldo. I could hardly sleep that night. I told myself that I was thirty-one years old, that it was time to forget about the old brown stuffed marine mammal. I told myself that if anyone could handle being lost in a strange city, it was my cool, calm, and collected Waldo. But none of this helped. The truth is, I was scared. I was scared, and I felt alone. I punched the pillow, wishing it were someone's guts. And then I froze. *Fight with words, and not fists*, a young voice whispered. In my tizzy, I had accidentally left a Lifetime movie playing on TV. But also, I had once written those words in my second-grade journal, so that Ms. Romanoff could read them. I ran to my laptop to compose one more email—an email using words instead of fists—to the Wynn Hotel's guest services department.

Monday morning finally dawned, and I stumbled out of bed, exhausted and delirious, crawling across the room to open my laptop. "Hello," an email from the Wynn Hotel began. "We are so glad to hear you enjoyed your visit. We were able to retrieve him! Waldo was in the linens with housekeeping. And we are happy to say that he is on his way home to you via UPS 2nd Day Air."

My mouth fell open. I raised my eyes to the ceiling and I began to cry. "Thank you very much for your prompt attention to this matter," I began to type in my response. And then I paused. That wasn't me. That's who I wanted the Wynn to think I was. The real me—the one who Waldo knew better than his own whiskers—was about to lose her mind from excitement. I deleted those words and began again. In the spirit of a young Jerry Glen, I decided to throw caution to the wind and just let my epidermis show.

"OMG," I replied to the do-not-reply email address. "Thank you, thank you, THANK YOU!!!!!" I went on to tell the story of Waldo, to review the highlights from my weekend in Vegas, and to briefly describe my vision for my wedding that summer. I was ecstatic, and I held nothing back.

I'm not quite sure what Ms. Romanoff and her dispassionate German baby would have made of this unrestrained, vulnerable exchange, and this time there was no elegant blue handwriting to give me a clue.

Gossip

Because I am on television, and because I was recently named a "Missouri native . . . an actress" by *Women's Running* magazine, I am officially "on the radar." Therefore, to satisfy the demands of hungry gossip-lovers everywhere, I will now present you with six stories about famous people I know or ran into once:

1) Gary Coleman

During spring break of sophomore year of college, my roommate Jo and I headed to Los Angeles for the first time. As two Midwesterners attending school on the East Coast, we were very excited about our maiden voyage to La La Land. We asked to stay with Jo's family friends, the Carltons, a gracious couple who served us sausage grinders and fried potatoes for dinner the night we arrived. It was a Friday during Lent, which for a Catholic like me means no meat, but I understood from The Baby-Sitters Club book series that California was very free-thinking (one of the Baby-Sitters, Dawn Schafer, hailed from Southern California and loved tofu and surfing at sunrise), so I decided to open my mind to new ideas and to sin.

The Carltons went to bed early but encouraged us to borrow their car and hit the town. Jo and I had no idea what hitting the town might entail, but down the street from the Carltons' house was a restaurant called Islands. The name alone had glamour written all over it, and we were ready to mix with the glitterati. I knew as soon as I walked through the door shaped like a palm tree that this was the real deal; blue neon lights screaming "Fine Burgers" and actual surfboards covering the walls assured me that this was not only a place to see, but also to *be seen*. A polite young woman showed us to a booth, and I remember thinking that, on her nights off from Islands, she was probably a music video star. Jo and I ordered some sundaes, even though I had given up ice cream for Lent, but remember that this was a new era of moral relativism for me.

As we put our menus down, a short African American man wearing an earpiece walked by, shouting, "Well, that's just not the sort of deal I'm interested in!" *Classic LA moment*, I thought to myself. *A movie agent, wheeling and dealing*. Our eyes met, and to my surprise, the man lowered the earpiece. "Is everything all right with you young ladies?" he asked. "Oh yes," I said. Jo nodded, adding, "We just ordered sundaes." I kicked her under the table. We were in Hollywood after all; did she want to go around announcing to everyone that we were pigs?!

The man removed his earpiece. "You two aren't from around here, are you?" I was shocked. This man was possibly one of the biggest movie agents in Hollywood, and he was talking to us, right here at Islands where, no doubt, so many had been discovered before. We chatted for a few minutes, and as the conversation was winding down, he smiled and reached out his hand. "Too bad we didn't meet earlier, when you were older," he said, shaking Jo's hand and then turning to me. "We could have dated."

And as I took this man's hand into my own, puzzling over his math that didn't quite check out, I recognized him perfectly: he wasn't a Hollywood movie agent at all. He was Gary Coleman. And he wanted to date me. Or Jo. He hadn't been clear.

2) Manohla Dargis (chief film critic for *The New York Times*)'s husband

When I ended up moving to LA at the age of twenty-nine, my then-agent and now-friend Priyanka invited my sister, Carrie, and me for drinks at a bar called Lou. We all sat down at the bar, and the bartender, who was opening a bottle of champagne, asked us what we would like. I ordered a glass of white wine, and as I finished speaking, the cork popped off the bottle, and the bartender accidentally sprayed about half of the champagne directly into my face. I waited for him to hand me a towel, or to apologize, or even to offer the rest of the bottle to me for free, but he did none of those things. As he left to pour the champagne into a flute, I turned to Priyanka. "Can you believe what just happened?" I asked her, seething. "He just sprayed champagne in my face!" "Shh," Priyanka shushed me. "Don't say anything. That's Manohla Dargis's husband. *That's Lou.*" I gave Priyanka one of my famous snorts and grabbed a napkin to start drying off. "Well, I don't know about Manohla," I grumbled to Carrie. "But this critic gives Lou one thumb down!" Carrie couldn't understand what I had said because I was grumbling so quietly, and that's too bad, because it was a pretty good line. Anyway, the point is, if you're in the market for a complimentary champagne shower and a truly fabulous cheese plank, head on over to Lou. (Please note: Lou is now closed, so I don't actually recommend this.)

3) Pope John Paul II

When I was eighteen and my brother Billy was nine, our mom somehow secured two tickets to a Mass being celebrated at the St. Louis Cathedral Basilica by Pope John Paul II. Since my older brother, John, was away at college (I was a college freshman on winter break), and Carrie had a geometry test that afternoon, Billy and I hopped in the family Chrysler minivan and drove downtown.

At the time, I was taking an introductory college course in Latin, and as soon as we were seated, I translated all the ceiling inscriptions to Billy, as though he were blind. I noticed, as I was finishing, that all the inscriptions were also written in English, just below the Latin—but still I knew that Billy appreciated the insight of a classics scholar such as myself. The Mass was beautiful but short, and as it drew to a close, hysteria quickly took over. People were jumping all over one another to try to touch the Pope as he made his recessional walk down the nave. I wished that everyone would quiet down and give the man some respect—but I also knew that if Billy and I missed an opportunity to touch this holy, healing man, I would never forgive myself. With a strength I can only explain as the Holy Spirit surging through me, I grabbed Billy and attempted to lift him to my shoulders. "What are you doing?" Billy protested, wresting himself from my rough, weathered hands. "Ellie, we don't need to touch him.

Leave the man alone!" The Holy Spirit ultimately failed me, and Billy sort of fell halfway into the pew in front of us. I yanked him back up and thrust him out toward the aisle. An elderly woman was in my way. "Excuse me," I barked at her, foam forming at the corners of my mouth. "Please make way for the child." The elderly woman wouldn't budge. Just then, the Pope glanced up at us, his head still bowed. Those clear blue eyes, the color of an Edenic pond, washed over me and I swear, I have never felt more at peace. Billy bowed his own head respectfully toward the Pope, and I quickly shoved Billy out of my way to try to catch a piece of the Pope's sleeve myself. "Ow!" my brother cried. "You're standing on my neck!" In the end, neither Billy nor I got to touch the Pope, but it doesn't really matter. I felt transformed, in a way that the elderly woman who wouldn't budge never could.

4) Gerard Butler

Last year, I was in line at a New York City West Village Starbucks for a nice dark roast, when I noticed a handsome man grinning wildly at nothing. This guy looked a lot like Gerard Butler, but I wasn't entirely sure, so I decided to snap a secret picture of him with my phone to text to my husband for confirmation. Just as I finished clicking, I heard a young gentleman behind me sigh. "Oh, come on," he said, his high-pitched voice peevish with unearned fatigue. "Can't you just let the poor guy *be*?" At first, I was incredulous. This Gerard Butler figure was looking all around the café, beaming as though there were magical elves as far as the eye could see. He didn't seem particularly concerned with going unrecognized. Then,

I grew furious. Since appearing on television, I occasionally notice people taking secret pics of me, and you know what I think? *Thank goodness someone's watching our show*. Then I think, *Wait a minute—is this another guy mistaking me for Danny Bonaduce?* Finally, I grew mortified. Why in the hell was I taking some sort of sick secret iPhone photo of Gerard Butler? Did the guy in line think I was going to masturbate to it later? I felt dizzy. I quickly put down my phone, walked backward out of the Starbucks so the guy in line couldn't see my face, and ran across the street (to the other Starbucks). The photo was blurry, but the memory is razor sharp.

5) Doris Kearns Goodwin

I am an enormous fan of Doris Kearns Goodwin; she is a brilliant historian whose body of work is breathtaking. More specifically, she puts current events in context and therefore makes me feel slightly less worried about the horrors of our modern world. We have been through this before, in other words, and we will go through this again, and as long as I have Ms. Goodwin to shine a light, I feel a little bit calmer.

So, when I caught sight of this woman at a party the year that the movie *Lincoln*, based on her book *Team of Rivals*, was an Oscar contender, I immediately went up to her. "I don't normally do this," I said, giving her one of my signature coy grins, "but I am an enormous fan and just wanted to tell you that." Doris Kearns Goodwin smiled brightly, and I leaned in, enthusiastically, to hug her. Unfortunately, she had begun to turn away by then, and—arms still outstretched—I lost my balance, stumbling forward and accidentally pushing the legendary biographer to the ground. "I'm so sorry," I muttered, my hot breath blowing over the back of her neck, my knee digging into her hamstring. I staggered to my feet, attempting to bring her up with me. "I didn't—I'm so sorry, Doris." My armpits began dripping with sweat, and I held a clawlike grip on the small woman's waist. I finally decided the most selfless thing I could do in that moment was simply run away from the situation entirely, and so I did. I can only imagine the portrait that Doris Kearns Goodwin might one day paint of me.

6) Ricky Gervais

I was at the 2010 Emmys along with the rest of the cast of *The Office*. It was my first awards show, and I was giddy. I wore a dark, forest-green strapless gown on loan from a place called Film Fashion, I had fake eyelashes, and my hairdresser had molded my hair into a Michael Pitt coif. I was owning life, and I had no reason to apologize. Then I met Ricky Gervais. "Oh my gosh!" I squealed. "It's so nice to meet you. I'm new on the show!" Ricky Gervais gave me a small, polite smile, and quickly nudged the woman he was with to keep walking. I wondered if I had overstepped a boundary; Ricky Gervais, of course, had created the British *Office*, but was I not supposed to speak to foreigners at an American awards show? It wasn't until the Governor's Ball, gnawing on room-temperature chicken satay and bloody filet mignon, that I learned Ricky Gervais had been spooked by our encounter. "What do you mean?" I asked B. J. Novak, who had relayed the news.

"He thought that you said, 'I'm *you* on the show,'" B.J. told me.

I was stunned. That sentence that B.J. had just repeated back to me didn't make any sense. "How could I think that I was *him* on the show?" I cried, beef blood dribbling down my chin. "Who could ever think that they are a different person than they actually are?" It occurred to me then that this very thing—thinking you are a different person than you actually are—is precisely what actors do on a daily basis. I suddenly felt like I was going to throw up, and I excused myself to the ladies' room, where I stuffed as many mini-hairsprays and lip glosses as I could into my borrowed Judith Leiber clutch, and then, head held high, made my way to the valet line.

Squirrel

As children, my three siblings and I were not allowed to see PG-13 movies, and the MPAA-sanctioned age of thirteen offered little hope. "It's not as though they are *advising* you to see the movie as soon as you turn thirteen," my mother told me, biting into a Hydrox. "It doesn't suddenly become *a good idea*." With such broken reasoning as this, I was forced to turn inward and listen to my own heart. More often than not, my heart told me to watch the forbidden film when my parents weren't around. I had seen heavy petting behind a pottery wheel during *Ghost* at Melissa Daniels's birthday sleepover when I was ten; I watched Sigourney Weaver get murdered by poachers in *Gorillas in the Mist* at Emily Sinclair's house on the night of fifth-grade graduation; *Beaches* I'd seen nearly half a dozen times, also at Emily's house—infidelity, drunkenness, and viral cardiomyopathies running wild. The one PG-13 movie that even my heart warned me against was *Dirty Dancing*. Frightened by the thought of never being able to erase those pornographic dance moves from my mind, I didn't dare attempt a viewing. As a young Catholic, I was terrified of sex. Kidnapped gorillas were one thing; Swayze's thrusting pelvis was quite another.

After an unlawful viewing of *Dances with Wolves* at Abby Marino's house in the fall of sixth grade, I knew immediately why this film had been slapped with its PG-13 rating: there is sex, and it is under a blanket. But that's not all. There is another scene where a fat, overheated major eats an enormous piece of cornbread, pees in his pants, and shoots himself. I heard soldiers cuss and I saw scalps get ripped off heads. This movie was all over the place in terms of sex, murder, and wolves; I knew that I shouldn't be watching it, and yet I couldn't bring myself to pretend to be asleep. In fact, none of the girls at Abby's house could tear their eyes away from the screen. We told ourselves that we were learning about history—but I think we all knew that we were in it for the horror. The slaughtered buffalo disgusted us, and we sobbed uncontrollably when Wind in His Hair professed his friendship love for Kevin Costner. I think we must have consumed three bags of Pop Secret during this viewing—looking back, I now see we were laying the groundwork for a lifetime of eating our feelings.

Grossed out by the behavior of the white men in the film, I grew excited by the idea that maybe one of my ancestors had been one of the first humans to cross the land bridge between Asia and North America. "Thousands of years ago," Mrs. Hutton told us in sixth-grade social studies, "Siberia was connected to Alaska, and this is how humans migrated to what is now America." I stared at her, my mouth agape. I raised my hand and asked her to repeat what she had just said. She told me to start listening more closely, because she would not be repeating herself. Anyway, was it possible that one of these land bridge migrators was a relative of mine?

When I floated this idea by my older brother, John, he laughed in my face. "How could you be a Native American?" he asked me. "Dad's family is German, and Mom's is Italian." I nodded as though I already knew that, my face growing a deep shade of red. I left the room with tears in my eyes, my blood boiling with the fiery tempers of the generations of angry German-Italians who had bequeathed it to me. What can I say? I was young and confused and *wanting to be anyone but me.*

Facts may have thrown me for a loop this time, but I resolved not to let the truth block my way entirely. There was a different, greater version of Ellie out there somewhere, and I had a feeling that I could find her somewhere in the movies. This was nothing new. Several years earlier, inspired by the modest clothing and pixie haircut of Fräulein Maria, I had explored the idea of becoming a nun-turned-governess. Alternatively, I had considered being accidentally left at home while the rest of my family went on a trip. I had even thought about getting really good at singing so that I could sell my voice for better legs. But I knew that I was too much fun to be a nun, too responsible not to set my alarm clock, and I already had amazing legs. Besides, now that I was watching more mature films than *The Sound of Music*, *Home Alone*, and *The Little Mermaid*, I figured that I could afford to aim a little bit higher. I didn't want to be a little troublemaking sneak who spilled Pepsi all over the table. I wanted to be someone who helped to make the world a better place.

And suddenly my new identity hit me like a ton of monkey dung: I would become Sigourney Weaver from *Gorillas in the Mist*.

I knew that I had to start communing with nature, effective immediately. Luckily, my dad had built us a tree house in our backyard years earlier, a very cool wooden fort with two floors and a rope ladder. I started going out to this tree house for hours on end. I wouldn't bring a book or a Walkman; I would simply sit on my bench and stare at the trees. Feeling alone in a human world that did not understand me, I sought refuge among the animals. You see, before my criminal run of PG-13 movies, I had enjoyed simpler pleasures—*Anne of Green Gables* and *The Secret Garden*. Before the name Sigourney Weaver had even entered my consciousness, I had gotten a kick out of Mary Lennox—why was she so grumpy?—but I had grown absolutely obsessed with the character of Dickon. I was fascinated by his ability to communicate with wildlife; nobody else I knew could hold prolonged eye contact with a robin. Plus, in the movie version, blackbirds sat on his shoulders and Dickon could walk on his hands. At one point, Dickon tells Mary Lennox that perhaps he *is* a bird or a fox or a squirrel, and that he just doesn't know it. I nearly shat my pants when I read that. Was it possible that I, too, was an animal?

On these outings, I would sit very still. I would even try to slow my breathing. If my foot fell asleep and I had to shift positions, I would do so at a glacial pace, because any sudden movements stood a chance of startling the creatures nearby. I would occasionally test God during these sessions. "God, if you exist," I would whisper, so softly I could barely even hear my own voice, "let a crow caw." If a bird, any bird, called out within five to twenty minutes of this appeal, I would smile gently and close my eyes, deeply content. God existed, all right.

There was one squirrel near the tree house, a fairly overweight squirrel, whom I nicknamed Natalie after a cute, chubby girl in my class. At first, I thought that Natalie might be more than one squirrel, and I just couldn't tell the squirrels apart; however, as an animal charmer—or possibly an animal myself—I wasn't about to tag these little guys. Also, no one at the hardware store had ever heard of "squirrel tags." I liked Natalie immediately. She moved at her own pace, and she was always eating. While I noticed that the other squirrels would often travel in groups of two or three, pausing to inspect a branch or some acorns before scampering away together, Natalie was always alone. She didn't really climb trees, and her pace could hardly be described as scampering; hers was more of a labored plod. Defying the lively dances of her fellow squirrels, Natalie lived her life one plunk at a time.

As the autumn wore on, I found myself settling deeper and deeper into the squirrel community. I started talking less, and squeaking more. I remembered an old rumor from kindergarten about Amy Martin's aunt; they said she had a tail. I wondered if that might just be where I was headed. I gradually learned to tell the differences among the animals, without the help of tags or nail polish. Patch, for example, had a small patch of white on his back. Ears had unusually large ears. Brownish was a little more brown than gray, and Tiny was very small. I giggled to myself, imagining the name they must have come up with for me. Was it Red Hair? Girl with the Great Legs? Saint Ellie?

One morning, I decided to feed Natalie. I knew that she liked food; now I wanted her to like *me*. Imagining that squirrels would have little interest in the man-made Wheat Thins and Magic Middles I found in my own pantry, I gathered some dry, black, withered berries from the dirt near the creek by our tree house. I was careful to go upstream of the sewer pipe that emptied directly into the water. I wasn't sure what these berries were—were they even berries at all?—but I reminded myself of Sigourney Weaver as I gathered them: a woman of great compassion born into a human family, slowly but confidently finding her true home among the animals. (I also didn't totally understand that Sigourney Weaver was playing the *character* of Dian Fossey; I would be lying if I said I don't still consider Ms. Weaver to be one of the foremost primatologists of our age.)

I found a large gray leaf and laid the shriveled berry-like scraps on them. I filled a shallow bowl with just a touch of creek water, set it next to the berries, and took my post on the bench.

Natalie didn't make an appearance for about an hour. This was not unusual; as I mentioned, Natalie didn't allow time to dictate her life. When I finally saw her tubby frame making its way through the brush, I looked away. I knew there was no chance that Natalie would come toward me if she thought that I was watching her. She wasn't the class clown; she wasn't a showboat. Natalie was just an obese squirrel trying to get through the day.

After a few moments, I gradually turned my head back to check on Natalie's whereabouts. I could not find her. I checked the berries: untouched. The bowl of creek water: still as the night. I momentarily forgot about moving slowly and leapt up. For as long as I had known Natalie, she had never, ever gotten from one place to another so quickly. I began to worry that something had eaten her while I was looking away. But what? Natalie was too heavy to be carried away by a crow, and too dumpy to be appealing to a coyote. I wasn't sure what to do.

I went down to the creek to clear my head. I knew that an animal lover like me could not control the free will of wild creatures; they were free to roam all the way to Warson Road and even up to Litzsinger, if that is what they wanted to do. But Natalie didn't have that kind of physical fitness, and so I felt anxious. I found a seat on Marriage Rock, a moss-covered boulder on which I sometimes acted out weddings with Carrie and Emily; I always played the groom. There was no cause for lifelong commitment vows on this occasion, however. Natalie was missing.

Directly across from Marriage Rock was a peculiar tree; it grew diagonally at a 45-degree angle, making it very easy to climb. There was even a thick vine that ran along its spine, aiding in a climber's quest to scale the trunk. Desperate for distraction, I got up and grabbed hold of the vine. Historically, a climber could take no more than about three or four steps before things got scary; your body would start to tilt at too steep an angle to feel secure, and the vine got thinner at the top. Ascending quickly, I had already reached this peak; I turned back to look at Marriage Rock.

Just as my gaze fell on the wedding moss, the vine snapped.

I began to free-fall, directly backward, heading straight for the shallow creek and its sharp rocks. There wasn't even enough water in the creek to make a splash; I landed hard on my back with a force that knocked the wind out of me. I lay there, unmoving, for what seemed like a minute. Miraculously, I didn't seem to be bleeding anywhere; I had managed to keep my head up when I hit the creek bed, thus avoiding any contact between the rocks and my skull.

I rubbed my eyes, stunned. I wasn't sure if I had died and come back to life. Had I spoken with any angels? I couldn't remember.

Then I heard a squeal that made my blood run cold.

I turned to look, and there was Natalie, an unearthly sound coming from her open mouth. It wasn't quite a scream, but it wasn't a cackle either; it was a shrill cry that reminded me of David Bowie's character from *Labyrinth*. Was Natalie laughing at me? Whatever she was doing, it seemed to be coming not from a place of fellowship, but of barbarity. Who was this unrecognizable brute, laughing in the face of my pain? I stared at Natalie, hurt and bewildered. This only seemed to make her laugh harder. I shook my head, tears welling in my eyes, unable to understand any of it.

I stood up and dusted myself off. Only the ankles of my jeans were damp, but I could explain it away as dew. I decided not to tell my mom what had happened; not only was I slightly embarrassed, but I feared that she would forbid me from going to the tree house by myself anymore. What if she made John accompany me? I winced, thinking of my big brother among the animals; he would probably try to blast Nirvana in an effort to get them to like him.

I trudged back up to the tree house, emptied the kitchen bowl, and began to make my way back to our house. I hoped that my mom hadn't been peeking out the window; I hoped no one else had seen what had just taken place. My backyard, once an oasis of unity and balance and creek water, now seemed fragmented, unkind.

In the lawless land of nature, as it turned out, it was every squirrel for herself.

Redhead

I knew not to take it personally when my driver's ed teacher, a soft-spoken elderly gentleman named Mr. Boehlow, told me that I frightened him. "My grandma taught me to beware of redheads," he said, gently pressing the passenger-side brake as I failed to press my own for the upcoming stop sign. "Granny said, 'Redheads *seem* nice, but redheads are witches.' " We came to a full stop and I pushed the gas pedal to move forward, but Mr. Boehlow wouldn't take his foot off his brake. He looked at me. "I'm scared of witches," he confessed.

Even at the young age of fifteen years and seven months, I understood that Mr. Boehlow was out of his mind. What was he talking about? I wasn't a witch. Witches were scary! I wasn't scary. Witches had cauldrons! I couldn't even boil pasta. Mr. Boehlow and his granny were way, way off base here—and yet, because I needed Mr. Boehlow to remove his birdlike foot from the brake, all I could do was chuckle politely and shake my head. "Don't worry, I'm not a witch," I said. "Unless witches now ride Dustbusters instead of brooms!" It wasn't true that I rode Dustbusters, but I definitely would reach for a Dustbuster over a broom in a crumb-cleaning situation, and so it felt close enough.

The truth is, I have always considered my mane of reddish-orange hair to be my greatest asset. I have really powerful quadriceps and very small ears, which I also love about myself, but my favorite feature is my red hair. Why wouldn't it be? It sets me apart from people who don't have red hair, and it instantly bonds me with people who do. Experts often say that redheads are an endangered species—but experts say a lot of things. My own hasty scans of sidewalks and shopping malls show plenty of us out and about. Maybe the experts are just saying that because they are jealous of all the redheads—and the only revenge they know is to claim that we will all die.

There is one unspoken rule among redheads, which is that we must immediately love one another. I knew before even reading the first page of Astrid Lindgren's classic that Pippi Longstocking was the girl for me. I understood that if I had been a scout in Shelley Long's Troop Beverly Hills, I would have been her favorite. Fräulein Maria, Caddie Woodlawn, Archie: these people all felt like family to me. The point is, redheads share a bond that remains unknown to blondes, brunettes, and babies who don't have hair yet. And I do not take this bond lightly.

I have changed the color of my hair just once in my life, and it was for work. On my first day as a cast member on *The Office*, I was asked if I wouldn't mind dyeing my hair to make it a bit darker. I said, "Yes!" But I didn't stop there. "Which way is the sink?" I added. Hello! This was my first job on a TV show, and not just any TV show—a really good TV show. I would have murdered someone if they had asked me to! No, I wouldn't have murdered anyone, but you get the idea. (I didn't murder anyone.)

The head of the hair department, Laverne, applied a temporary brown color to my hair, and at lunch, I saw Mindy Kaling. "Whoa," she said. "Did you dye your hair?" I told her that some of the producers had asked me to darken it because it looked too similar to Pam's on camera. "You're a good sport," she replied.

"I would not dye my hair if someone told me to." From bringing over cake to celebrate my first appearance on *Craig Ferguson* to always greeting my parents with a hug to dressing up in gold lamé with me simply because we *could*,[1] Mindy Kaling is a classy-ass woman who was raised right. So I trust her instinct not to let others tell her what to do. But as a redhead, I was accustomed to being in a position where I couldn't necessarily negotiate. Let me elaborate.

Even though I see my red hair as a blessing, I think we all know by now that with every blessing comes a curse. In fourth grade, when Christopher Holmes told everyone at our lunch table which kind of dog they would be, I was the Irish setter. "And nobody ever wants an Irish setter," he added, smirking. "Because they shed," he explained. I nodded at the time, but that was only because I wasn't sure what we were talking about. Was it still dogs? When Miss Betty would drop me off at the front of my lane after school, she'd call out, "See ya, Red Top!" and all the kids on the school bus would laugh. "Red Top! Red Top! Red Top!" they would chant. I would turn around and laugh, too, but only because I wanted George Watkins, the youngest of all the Watkins brothers—and also the cutest!—to see what a great smile I had. Why did the children chant at me? I would later come to see that sometimes people are intimidated by that of which they are envious. In these situations and others like them, I had to swallow my pride and hold my red head high, and so when Laverne from the hair trailer summoned me, I humbly complied.

I enjoyed being a brunette for the six weeks that I was film-

1 As members of our fictional girl band, Subtle Sexuality. Look it up and thank me later!

ing. By the time we wrapped, the dye had pretty much faded, and I was back to my usual hue. But I noticed something about myself during my dance with brown hair. I was not quite the carefree, happy-go-lucky sweetie pie I used to be. I wasn't *severe*, exactly. I was just a tad more serious. I often found myself cocking my head to the side and saying, "Huh." I contemplated my daily interactions slightly more deeply. I ruminated. Once, I found myself with Rebecca West's *Black Lamb and Grey Falcon* in my hands. I quickly realized I had been using it to prop up my pad Thai container so I didn't need to lean down as far while watching *The Comeback*, but still, I could tell I was becoming much more focused.

I also noticed that I couldn't get away with as much. If I was eating at a restaurant, no longer did my girlish giggles aid me in my quest for free dessert. "Would you like any coffee or tea?" the waiter would ask. I would then smile and say there was no way I could possibly have dessert. "I'm already about to bust my pants as it is!" I would squeal. "Okay," the waiter would reply. And then he would bring the check. *Hey, where's the brûlée?* I would think to myself, using my shorthand for "crème brûlée."

Small children didn't laugh at me anymore. "Look out for the crazy cardinal!" I would shout, pretending to fly into a window and fall down. My godson would remain unimpressed. "I think he wants you to read to him," his mom would whisper to me. I no longer worried about wearing certain shades of hot pink, bartenders weren't charmed when I ordered a Shirley Temple, extra grenadine, and my agents started sending me out for more lawyer roles. In any case, my time as a brunette wasn't exactly profound, but it taught me a lot of things about being a different kind of white person.

My return to being a redhead was predictably triumphant. And yet, sometimes I find myself enjoying my red hair so much that I forget the concept of moderation. In 2012, the cast of *Bridesmaids* was invited to present several awards at that year's Oscars. I knew that I might never get this kind of historic opportunity again, so I decided to pull out all the stops. I hired a stylist who helped me find a gorgeous Giorgio Armani Privé dress. (A Privé dress is different from a regular Armani dress because it has the word *Privé* at the end.) I went on a juice cleanse for the three days leading up to the ceremony to ensure that my blood would be 70 percent kale. I plucked all hairs, I scrubbed all skin, and I even visited a Reiki healer with the hope that she would heal the tingling cystic acne threatening to burst forth and ravage my jawline just in time for Oscar night. But the one thing I did not do was cut my bangs. They were on the longish side, but I thought this could only work in my favor. My Privé dress was a gorgeous shade of copper (I had first described it as "rust" but was sternly reprimanded by my stylist), and I figured the longer my own copper bangs, the greater the copper sensation.

There was only one drawback to these long bangs, and that was that I couldn't see. I wasn't blind; the length wasn't completely blocking my sight. But I would estimate that the top quarter of my line of vision was cut off by a blunt layer of red. "I am so excited to be here!" I told Ryan Seacrest's chin. "I can't believe I just got out of a car and someone said, 'Welcome to the Academy Awards.' It's surreal!" Ryan Seacrest made some pleasant conversation back to me, which I knew because most of what I could see of his face were his lips, and then I moved along to the next interview.

I clung to my fiancé Michael's arm closely, not only because it was an incredibly special night to share as a couple, but also because I had no peripheral vision:

This photo was taken during the portion of the evening where all the actors take off their clothes. I'm kidding! You just can't see my dress because it was strapless. And you also can't see any cystic chin acne because the Reiki lady healed it!

Backstage at the Oscars, the cast of *Bridesmaids* and I were getting ready to present the awards for Best Live Action Short, Best Documentary Short Subject, and Best Animated Short Film. As I sat on a couch, reading over my lines on a blue index card, I suddenly heard a voice that could only be described as belonging to Captain von Trapp. And that, my friend, is because the voice belonged to Captain von Trapp. Christopher Plummer from *The*

Sound of Music was standing directly across from me, and when I heard his voice, my head shot up so quickly that my bangs parted, revealing him to me without obstruction. This man was asking for a glass of water, and I knew immediately what I had to do. I put down the index card, ran to the bar, and demanded a glass of water, no ice. *Why all the fuss?* you might be asking. *The guy just wanted some water.* You pause. *And why no ice?* I do not have an answer for your second question, but I do for your first. Of the billions and billions of men in this world, you see, Captain Georg Ludwig Ritter von Trapp was the very first on whom I ever had a crush. Not the real guy, of course. I refer to, instead, the movie guy portrayed by Arthur Christopher Orme Plummer in 20th Century Fox's 1965 epic Alpine musical. This Captain von Trapp was everything my seven-year-old self was ever looking for in a man: tall, handsome, and not too proud to sing "Edelweiss." And even though I was engaged to be married the following July, I still held a special place for the Captain in my heart. This is why, when I heard his regal request for a glass of water, I sprinted to the bar as fast as my Naired legs could carry me.

Unfortunately, as I ran back across the room with a wineglass of room-temperature water, I failed to see a makeup chair to my left and so I tripped over its foot. I went down, like a robin with a bum wing, my fall broken only by the calf of a greenroom aide. Miraculously, no one saw this fall except for the greenroom aide and me. "Are you okay?" he asked politely. I looked up but could only see his neck. "Thank you," I said. "I wasn't sure if Plummer needed some water." When I rose to my feet, I brushed my bangs away from my eyes, and I saw that the Captain was no longer in the room. I turned to the aide, whose credential tag read "Mark." "Well, Mark," I said, arranging my bangs so that I was blind again, "I guess this one's for me." I chugged the iceless water down in about fifteen seconds flat, and then I raised the empty glass. "Pour one out for the Captain," I added, inaccurately, as I had just drunk all the water.

There is really just one disadvantage to being a redhead, and that is the widely held belief that we are temperamental sprites who are quick to anger. Often, in interviews, reporters will ask me if I have a bad temper. They ask me this partly because I portray happy, optimistic ladies on television, but mostly because I have a big face with orange hair. These reporters want to know *what makes the clown cry*. "What pisses you off?" a man from *GQ* asks, and I can almost hear his sneaky grin spreading over the phone. *"What makes Ellie Kemper mad?"* "Well," I answer tightly. "I guess that I get in bad moods just like anyone else." I pause before masterfully guiding the conversation back to the project at hand. "Anyway, I wasn't actually burping in that episode of *Kimmy Schmidt*; they added those burps in postproduction. And I think that the burps are very important because—"

"But what makes you *seethe?*" he goes on, undeterred. *"What makes this redhead fly off the handle?"* I take a deep breath and remind myself that not all redheads have fiery tempers. *You're not a fiery one*, I tell myself. *L. Ron Hubbard was a redhead, but that doesn't mean you have to fly off the handle as often as he did.*

You're the Amelia Earhart kind of redhead, I add. (The *GQ* writer interrupts my thoughts to ask if I'm still on the line. I tell him that I am.) *You're the free-spirited kind from the Midwest who loves new challenges*, I continue to think to myself. I smile and announce to the *GQ* writer that I am ready to proceed with the interview. *But you don't go missing over the Pacific!!!!* I silently remind myself, just in time.

"I get mad when people don't have good manners," I say calmly.

I can hear the reporter catch his breath. "Like what kind of bad manners?" he asks. He is so pleased because he believes that he has won! "I think we had better stop talking about me flying off the handle," I hiss. I kick the table leg of whatever table I'm sitting at, hitting my shin, which will then bruise even more deeply than if I were not a redhead, because redheads bruise more easily than other people.

I thank the reporter for his time, and then I hang up the phone. *That was easy*, I think to myself. And then I wonder if Julianne Moore would ever want to be automatic friends with me.

Redheads for the win!

Boss

Every year at Christmas, my younger sister, Carrie; our next-door neighbor Emily; my younger brother, Billy (from the age of two and three quarters on); and I would mount a holiday theatre piece in my family's front hall. The evening consisted of a moralistic play and a festive dance performance, followed by a kitchen reception with homemade cookies and tap water. I don't know why we didn't serve hot cocoa or milk.

These shows took years off my life. And yet, when people ask me why I needed to do them, why I felt this obligation, I simply shrug. "Why did Van Gogh cut off his ear?" I reply, not really wanting an answer. My point in bringing up Van Gogh's ear is that artists are out of their minds, and genius can't be explained. That's as good a reason as I can give.

As the oldest sibling involved with the process—and even older than Emily by sixteen days—I knew that I was the only one in the group responsible enough to pull off both a show and a kitchen reception of this caliber. As a result, I was not only the director, the line producer, the costume designer, and the prop master, but also an actor, writer, and dancer. I was the quintessential multi-hyphenate before I had all my adult teeth. Of course, while juggling all of this, I was also expected to shoulder the normal amount of elementary school and, in later years, junior high school coursework. To put it bluntly, ten hours of sleep was a good night—and that's if I was lucky. Every year I would tell myself that this was the last year. And every year a voice would whisper to me quietly but firmly: *You owe it to the fans.*

Just who were these fans? They were a devoted crew, making up in loyalty what they may have lacked in number. They consisted of Emily's dad, Dr. Sinclair, a white-haired ophthalmologist who, for several months in 1987, I believed had played the Steve Martin role in *Roxanne*; Emily's mom, Mrs. Sinclair, a petite, fit woman who had three jock sons in addition to Emily; my own mom and dad; and my maternal grandma and grandpa. I knew that our Christmas performance had the power to make or break these people's holiday season, and so year after year, I would sacrifice my own yuletide comfort for the sake of art.

Early in September, Emily, Carrie, and I would gather around the enormous IBM computer in a nook just off my parents' bedroom. Emily and Carrie would usually gab about that week's *Golden Girls* as I pounded away at the keyboard, fueled by a mix of excitement, dread, and cortisol. KeyWords, our school's computer keyboarding tutorial, was a program that I had aced. But even the satisfaction that I derived from my insane typing skills was not enough to make up for the fact that I was doing most of this on my own.

One year, little seven-month-old Billy was still sleeping in that master bedroom nook; having to schedule our writing sessions around his naps was just another burden that I alone had to bear. I was already working around Emily's weekly Girl Scout meetings, Carrie's biweekly gymnastics classes, and my own annual pizza-making Saturday. (Every year, Conway School sold frozen pizzas to raise money for the school, and students could volunteer to help; all volunteers received a free large cheese pizza. I usually took the morning shift.) My Baby-Sitters Club wall calendar was dog-eared almost beyond recognition—rehearsals, conflicts, and Pizza Saturday written, erased, crossed out, and rewritten.

As all directors must, I had to learn how to manage my actors early on. There was no class I could have taken on this; blogs and social media didn't exist. Instead, like a sort of artsy Lewis and Clark, I was forced to navigate my own way. Of course, I had no Sacagawea to provide clarity or context, nor did I have a Seaman[1] to keep me company. I was a one-woman Lewis and Clark expedition—and I was determined to reach the Pacific Ocean.[2]

Experience alone would teach me that the key to managing your actors is to understand your actors. Carrie, for example, was reliable, diligent, and prepared. I could count on her to have lines memorized and to stand where she was supposed to stand, give a confused look when the script instructed her to do so, etc. I didn't need to worry about Carrie being late or missing a rehearsal; my younger sister took direction well and adjusted her performance accordingly. "Carrie," I would rasp, sipping a hot chocolate long ago grown cold, "remember where your character is *emotionally* at this point." I walked over to Carrie and pretended to examine her clip-on earring. "Focus on the sacrifice," I whispered quickly, then resumed my perch in an old rocking chair. I understood that a director is most effective when communicating directly with the actor, out of earshot of the rest of the cast. Rocking back and forth slowly, I looked at Carrie meaningfully. *You know what to do*, said my eyes. "ACTION!" said my voice.

1 Newfoundland dog who accompanied Lewis and Clark on their expedition in a pet capacity.

2 My editor suggests this might be enough already with the Lewis and Clark comparison, but I disagree.

Carrie gazed at the Christmas tree. "Mom? Are you in the kitchen?" she asked bravely. Her chin quivered, but her eyes were steady. I nodded. Carrie Kemper was a good horse to have in my stable.

Emily Sinclair was more of a wild stallion. I knew that every horse could be tamed, but I also knew there was a reason cowboys drank. I learned early on that mercurial actors like Emily don't want to do as they are told. "Emily," I would say brightly, "I love what you are doing with that Tamagotchi! Aw, crud. There's no place to put the Tamagotchi! I think we have to take it out of the scene." Emily's brow would furrow, and her face would grow stormy. "What if we just *put it on the table*?" she would snap, angry that it was 9:00 on a Saturday morning and she was stuck at rehearsal instead of sleeping in. What Emily didn't know was that I had secretly *wanted* her to put the Tamagotchi on the table all along!

Billy Kemper was a breeze when he was cooperating, but a real pain when he was going pooh[3] in his diaper. I realized that I had to be gentle when working with child actors, but still, it grew tiresome. "Billy?" I would call out, exasperated. "Your dance number is up, Billy!" My dad would call back from the basement. "Bill and I are building a train!" I would throw down my script. Carrie would look scared, and Emily would continue filing her nails. "When's lunch?" she would ask, blowing another Bubblicious bubble and popping it in Carrie's face.

Late one Friday evening, I was pulling costume options from the large cardboard dress-up box in my closet. The box was on a shelf just beyond my reach, but instead of grabbing a chair to stand

3 Traditionally, this word appears as "poo" in writing. I have always thought this spelling looks way too cute for the substance it describes. And so I choose a more robust spelling, with an "h" at the end: "pooh."

on, I jumped up several times, pushing the box at a diagonal until it was teetering off the edge. Groaning with the weight of sequined skirts, Santa beards, princess crowns, tap shoes, silk scarves, and various men's jackets, the box began to slide off the shelf. I tried to catch it, but it was no use. The box knocked me to the floor. I lay trapped under its weight, my Cherokee jeans peeking out from under the mess of feathers and corduroy. "Carrie!" I cried out, my own voice muffled. "Emily!" I said more softly, already beginning to relinquish hope. Out of the corner of my eye, a disposable camera flashed, accompanied by a chorus of girlish giggles.

As the great Rodney Dangerfield used to joke, *I wasn't getting any respect.*

The year Emily and I were in sixth grade and Carrie was in second, our play was called *Christmas Magic*. This dramedy followed the story of the Tilken family, a single mother (played by me) and her two daughters, Ashley and Samantha (played by Carrie and Emily), living somewhere vaguely in the Midwest. In our plays, I always played the mom, and the mom was always single. Because Emily was tall, could do a deep voice well, and sometimes had short hair, I often encouraged her to expand her range by tackling a male character—but she refused. And so, our plays were dominated by strong female types; zero mention was ever made of the absent fathers and husbands. Years earlier, in a rare summertime production, we presented a drama called *Who Are You, Mr. Baby?* My character's pregnancy was explained away as an actual visit from the stork; it was, my character insisted, a real-life avian miracle.

What can I tell you? We're women. Our choices are never easy.[4]

4 *Titanic*, obviously.

Christmas Magic took on another miracle, but this time, it was of the holiday variety. The Tilken family had always made each other homemade gifts for Christmas; Mrs. Tilken would supplement with presents from Santa, of course, but the point was that gifts should be from the heart. Suddenly, innocence is shattered when Ashley finds out that her older sister has gone ahead and purchased a hair dryer, an electric nail dryer, and a see-through phone as gifts for her family members. Stunned, Ashley feels that her own homemade cards will never measure up. That night, she confides in her diary that she will replace the cards with various high-end items from around her own bedroom. She will give her mother her Skip-It, and her older sister her crimper. She will also give her older sister her unopened bottle of Debbie Gibson's fragrance, Electric Youth, as a stocking stuffer. Then, Ashley Tilken rips up her homemade cards.

Magic visits the household on Christmas morning when the family opens their presents to reveal *the original homemade cards perfectly intact*. These were, as it turned out, the gifts that Ashley Tilken was always meant to give. They were the gifts from her heart.

The days and nights leading up to Opening Night and Closing Night (the same night) of *Christmas Magic* were predictably hellish. Emily didn't know her lines; Billy couldn't remember any of the dance moves. Carrie was on time and helped with costume design, but I was sharing her with the YMCA gymnastics instructors in Kirkwood—and it often felt like they were winning. As for me, I was getting by on nine hours of sleep a night and my body was beginning to feel it. I was downing what must have been five mugs of Swiss Miss a day, but I was too preoccupied to recognize that I might be developing a problem.

As our play opened on the evening of December 21, 1991,

the audience was rapt. The lights came up, and small, delicate flakes of snow began to flutter down upon Ashley Tilken and her best friend, Beth Anderson (played by tall Emily Sinclair on her knees), as they walked home from school. The young girls have just been let out for Christmas vacation, and their excitement is palpable. "Two weeks of vacation!" sighs Ashley happily. As with so much of this show, you could not see me in this scene—*but you could see my invisible hand in the work*. Silently squatting on our second-floor landing, I threw fistfuls of white construction paper scraps from a brown Shop 'n Save grocery bag onto the scene below. I could take little delight in the twirling, glimmering spectacle; there was a music cue halfway through the scene that I needed to listen for. "Let's stop in this store for some candy canes" was the line right before I needed to press Play on the tape recorder for "It's Beginning to Look a Lot Like Christmas." Because our tape recorder didn't really amplify beyond ten feet, we had to keep it close to the audience. But the audience was down below, and I was up above. Therefore, upon hearing my cue, I would need to race to the other side of the landing, down the stairs (dressed in all black to avoid attention), across the stage to the tape recorder, and then up to the landing again, all the while *not allowing a break in the snow*. Were I to make the cue *precisely* on time, there would still be a microscopic lull in the flakes. That was a *best-case* scenario. There was zero room for error.

"It's snowing!" my grandma exclaimed.

My grandma had chosen her moment poorly. She stepped on Emily's line, arguably the most important line of the play: "Ashley, I can't wait to see the homemade cards that you made for your family this year." I was a tad, ah, *frustrated* with my grandma. *We see that it's snowing*, I thought to myself on the second-floor landing, sweat dripping from inside my black mask, paper cuts on my fingers bloodying the snow. *Now stop yakking so everyone else can follow the story.*

"Do you see the snow, Billy?" my grandma called out to my younger brother. Billy was seated on my dad's lap; he wouldn't be making an appearance until after intermission, in the Holiday Dances portion of the evening.

"Shhhhhh," I muttered from the landing. "There's a show going on." But it was no use. You couldn't hear my muffled voice behind the mask.

"Yeah, let's go in the store!" Carrie, as Ashley Tilken, agreed. *Holy Mother of God*, I thought. *I missed my cue!!!* I threw the paper bags up in the air, raced down the stairs, and ran across the front hall to press Play on the tape recorder. Both paper bags came sailing to the floor just as "Everywhere you goooo" blared out. I had accidentally thrown the bags over the banister! I quickly gathered them and began to run back up the stairs, but my mask had fallen down over my eyes; I couldn't see my way and I suddenly began to tumble backward down the stairs. When I landed on the stage, the snow was all around me; Carrie Kemper, bona fide pro, didn't miss a line. "If we get two candy canes," she explained to Beth, "we can get the third one for free!" I knew at that point I needed to get off the stage as quickly as possible. The show must—and would—go on.

"Billy, is the snow cold?" my grandma asked.

The rest of the play somehow proceeded smoothly. To be perfectly honest, the only major snag was when an actor forgot a line—and that actor was me. It happened during the debut of my character, Mom, vacuuming the living room in a button-down shirt and jeans. "Mom, why aren't you at work?" exclaimed Ashley. The lack of sleep combined with the nasty fall I had just taken down the stairs had turned my brain to mashed potatoes. I paused. "Hello," I said to Carrie. Carrie's eyes grew wide. She knew that was not my line. "Well, Carrie—" This time, Carrie and I both froze. I had done the unimaginable; I had broken the fourth wall. This was a disaster.

But in disasters are artists made.

"Well, Carrie . . ." I repeated. "Well, Carrie . . . is my boss at work," I went on, not quite sure of the words coming out of my own mouth, but positively exhilarated to find that they were, "and she announced that today is the first day of our vacation, too." Carrie's gasp was audible. I never broke eye contact with her. I had taken a nightmare mistake, the kind you only read about in books, and I had righted the course. "Look at all the candy canes I bought with Beth!" Carrie said, continuing the scene. We smiled at each other. Not with our mouths. We smiled at each other with our eyes.

They say that the universe never gives you more than you can handle, and I find myself wanting to believe that. But that year's Christmas Play and Dance would be my fourth to last. Our lives were getting busier, and in our later years, I began to recognize that I could no longer deliver a product that I believed in. Also, several critics had gently suggested moving on from the front-hall productions now that I was old enough to be getting my driver's license the following May.

Did I feel the added pressure of delivering a top-notch show because I was a woman? Of course I did. As unfair as it sounds, if anyone were to give my show a thumbs-down, it would make it harder for women of future generations to have the opportunity to make good Christmas shows. It would be another twenty years before "Should more women be directing and producing in Hollywood?" became a popular question on the red carpet at the

Kids' Choice Awards. Of course, women like Dorothy Arzner, Ida Lupino, Susan Harris, and I had been directing and producing before those kids even knew what green slime was.

The point is, sometimes it's good to be in charge. But also, sometimes it's less stressful not to have to do all that work.

Jock

In high school, I played field hockey in the fall and ran track in the spring. Simply put, I was a jock. I embraced this label for many reasons. First, it made me sound strong and rugged. Second, it put people around me at ease, as if they could sense my ability to protect them from potential bullies. Finally, it ensured that I would never, ever, not in a million years, be mistaken for a wimpy little nerd!

As far as field hockey identities go, I took mine pretty seriously. When preseason started, in mid-August, I made sure to show up to practice early and sweaty. To accomplish this, I would do jumping jacks on our driveway while I waited for my dad to take me to school. If asked, I would tell my coach that I had begun my warm-up at home—it was, after all, never too early to get better. I needed her to know not only that I was a responsible kid who understood the importance of being on time, but also that whatever I may have lacked in technical skills, I could more than make up for in dampness.

On game days in high school, it was traditional for sports teams to wear their jerseys to class. I adored both the design (KEMPER in bold gold or bold navy, depending on whether the game was at home or away) and my number (25—a nice square number that called to mind great things, like Christmas and manganese). But

I didn't stop at my jersey. I would often produce my stick after lunch on a game day, calling out to any teammates who happened to be sitting nearby in the student lounge. "Wolfe!" I'd shout, using a deeper voice than usual. "Let's drill!" Sandy Wolfe would look up from her physics textbook and frown. *Nerd!* I thought. I'd shove my mouth guard on my upper teeth, take a tennis ball over to the area by the PE offices, and start hitting it against a brick wall. Coach Keefer would run out and yell at me to stop, but I could tell she was impressed by my grit. I removed my mouth guard and spat on the carpet. *I am a sports monster*, I would think to myself.

I began my freshman year at Princeton in 1998 as a member of the field hockey team. Though the coach had not actively recruited me, she had given me her official support when it came time for admissions; if the admissions committee had been on the fence about letting me in, her support could have tipped the scales in my favor. Additionally, if I were accepted, I wouldn't have to try out for the team; I was already guaranteed a spot.

College promised to take my athletic intensity to a new level. Princeton was a Division I school, which is the highest level of intercollegiate sports. The field hockey team had competed for the national title in four of the last five NCAA Semifinals before I got there, and we ended up coming in second in the nation during my freshman year. As a sports monster, I felt ready. I had followed the training manual all summer (for the most part).[1] I

1 I avoided the weight-lifting portions of the regimen because, in the summer, teachers suddenly started coming to the student weight room. Seeing teachers sweating in their shorts and glimpsing their exposed calves was disorienting and I wanted nothing to do with it. Instead, I waited until the Sunday before I left for college and went through every exercise in the training manual exactly twice. I ended up spraining my shoulder because I lifted more than two hundred weights that day, but at least I knew how the weight machines worked.

ran long distances or did sprints according to that day's instructions; I arranged pickup games of field hockey whenever I could. I attended field hockey camps at Duke and Northwestern, and I studied the Princeton player profiles obsessively. These players became celebrities in my mind before I ever met them: Sadie Beck, Meghan Pizer, Layla Martin. I memorized all their stats and hometowns. When I actually saw them in person, I was starstruck. I remember not being able to speak in front of Sadie. Hers was the trajectory I aspired to have; she arrived her freshman year from upstate New York and skyrocketed to team MVP almost immediately. She was also drop-dead gorgeous. She had beautiful blond hair, a toothpaste-commercial smile, and legs that wouldn't quit. My own legs have never been described as "not quitting" so much as "unusually dry," but I knew it didn't matter. Sadie and I had one thing in common: we were both sports monsters.

As the first day of college preseason—with its numerous wind sprints, endless dribbling, and one acutely distressing stadium-climb session—finally drew to a close, I realized I had undertaken the greatest physical challenge of my life. I wasn't tired, exactly. Rather, I felt "off," in the sense that I could no longer feel my limbs or control my breathing. It wasn't mere fatigue, and it wasn't quite nirvana; I could hear my heart racing, so I also knew it wasn't death. Yet even in that strange state, overcome with new sensations and a sudden inability to swallow, I understood that it was of the utmost importance to continue appearing tough. I could see Layla Martin taking off her shin guards nearby. "Kim?" I loudly asked a freshman whose name tag read "Kim." I mopped some sweat off my brow and once again deepened my voice. "Just curious, any idea if these ladies do a cool-down, like a half-mile, or a mile, or what have you?" Kim shrugged, but I felt confident that Layla had overheard me asking for more work. I spat on the turf and gave Kim a salute before trotting off toward the track. Then I fell down, because my legs could no longer physically support the weight of my body. "Guess I'd better stretch," I called out, to no one.

The one thing I could do really well was run fast. In fact, I think that our coach—a long, lean woman named Kelly Troy—liked me mostly *because* I could run fast. A runner herself, Kelly had undergone nearly a dozen knee replacement surgeries on her left knee, or so the legend went. To me, Kelly seemed like a pretty standard college coach. She did not smile very much, she wore mirrored sunglasses all the time, and she was incredibly tan. I liked Kelly. Over the course of my life, I have been shaped by a parade of inscrutable men, and Kelly Troy was no exception. I never knew exactly where I stood with her, but for the most part, I didn't mind. I think it's good to be a little scared of your boss. I also think people who like running like other people who like running.

It wasn't too long before I began to settle into preseason. At night, the other freshmen and I would go to Pizza Colore and eat our weight in calzones. Since school had not officially started, the campus was filled only with athletes, and it felt cool to be a part of this hearty gang of sports players. I quickly fell in love with five different soccer players as we passed the men's team on the way to and from practice every morning. I could tell by the way they never looked at me that these guys talked about me in the locker room, but I tried to act like it was no big deal. It was an innocent time when only jocks roamed the Earth, working hard during the day and then enjoying reasonably priced and highly caloric Italian food at night.

There were just two issues keeping me from loving preseason

with all of my heart, and one of them was the fact that I was not one of the top players on the team. This was a strange feeling, because I was used to being a total sports monster. I had always known that stick skills and technical abilities were not my strong suits; instead, I tended to fudge my way through games by running fast. While this tactic might not work for more polished sports like golf or ballet, it seemed to work just fine for field hockey. I think that what a person lacks in finesse, she can often make up in hustle—and running is something that you can just keep doing and doing until you get faster.[2]

The other issue was the communal shower. I had never taken a shower with other women before. In fact, I had never taken a shower with anyone before. In my high school locker room, as in my childhood home, we had individual showers; if you found yourself wanting to take showers with others in either place, you had to actively make it happen. In college, there was both a communal shower *and* individual showers; however, only the goalie ever showered alone. I always tried to smile at Clara as she made her way past the big showers and into the lonely stall. *Come on*, I said with my eyes. *Come on in to the big showers with the naked field hockey players so it won't be weird.* I found Clara's voluntary isolation devastating. It wasn't cool to opt for the individual shower; the implication was either that you had something to hide or that you were uncomfortable with naked women. Both of these things were (and are) true for me, but I wasn't about to do anything to stand out from the crowd.

2 The other thing that I had on my side were my quads. For reasons inexplicable, I have always had enormous quadriceps muscles. This gives me the appearance of being incredibly strong, and it frightens opponents. In fact, my quadriceps muscles are *so* enormous and iron-like that on a 1990 summer vacation to Florida when I was only ten years old, my older brother, John, gave me the nickname "Quadzilla."

The first time I saw Meghan Pizer with no clothes on, I almost fainted. This was like seeing Julia Roberts at a gynecologist appointment, or Sandra Bullock in the Loehmann's shared dressing room. I never knew where to look during these shower sessions; I just tried to get in and out as fast as possible and could not understand how some of the seniors simply stood there, not moving, closing their eyes, and letting the water pour over them after a difficult practice. Who were these brave women, and where was their shame?

Most shocking to me was the pubic hair—or, shall I say, the *lack thereof*. As a Catholic teenager from the Midwest, I had been unaware that pubic hair served any purpose other than to catch flies before they reached my vagina. Well, it turned out that a lot of women opt to eliminate their pubic hair entirely. I unexpectedly found myself as the earthy, hippie flower child among a sea of Barbies. *Free love*, I may as well have shouted from my crotch. *Let it flow*. Even if I *had* wanted to blend in and groom my bikini area, I had no idea how to even go about such a thing. Did they go to a doctor? Did they do it themselves? I was terrified by the idea of taking a pair of scissors to such a precious region, and so I alone remained unshorn and untamed. Suddenly, I understood why Clara might have preferred to shower by herself.

As preseason drew to a close, and late summer turned to early fall, I quickly learned that I would not be seeing much playing time. For the first few games, I held out hope; I assumed that it was just a matter of paying my dues, and that of course the upperclassmen should get first dibs. Kelly probably needed a strong leader on the bench to keep the team motivated, I told myself. I knew that a sports monster could wear all sorts of hats, even that of benchwarmer. Nonetheless, as September progressed and I continued to warm the bench, I started to worry. Every single other freshman began to see playing time. Sometimes it was only for five or six minutes, but it spoke volumes to me. I was clearly the worst player on the team!

At first I was mad. On its very small and very specific level, this treatment was humiliating. *You can still run fast*, I would encourage myself. *But you're not as skilled as the other players, and your pubic hair is five times as long*. Then, my anger turned into an obsession with watching sports movies: *The Cutting Edge*, *A League of Their Own*, *Rudy*. And it was during my dozenth or so viewing of *Rudy* that I made a decision. Just as Rudy finally got his chance to shine after nearly giving up, I decided to plead with my field hockey coach to give me some playing time.

And so, early one fall morning, as dawn broke over Nassau Street, I psyched myself up by doing a round of push-ups in the hall bathroom. (My roommate, Jo, was still sleeping and I didn't want to wake her.) I got dressed and headed to Kelly Troy's office. She wasn't there, so I jogged around the gymnasium a couple of times. I did a few squats and started in on some burpees. The janitor asked me to leave just then, but I could see the light was now on in Troy's lair. I thanked the janitor and got ready to make history.

Kelly Troy's door was closed, and I knocked softly. She didn't hear me, so I knocked again. "Come in!" she barked. "I already said, 'Come in!' " I guess she had heard me the first time. Anyway, she was at her desk doing paperwork, still wearing her mirrored sunglasses. Only then did I realize that they must be prescription glasses. *I wonder why she doesn't get glasses that aren't sunglasses*, I thought. But I quickly regained my focus. I sat down, and Kelly removed her sunglasses. In that moment, I felt the exact same way as I do whenever I take off my socks: something about this was wrong. I had never seen Kelly's eyes before, and I froze. Then I took a deep breath, and I looked the woman in the eye. I was able to get a sense of her soul.

I explained to Kelly that I was concerned about my progress on the team. I had noticed that I was the only player who had never played in a game, and I thought that might be a bad sign. Kelly leaned back in her chair and crossed her legs. The knee of a thousand replacements was on full display. I wasn't sure if this was a power move. "Ellie," she said, in a voice that was kind but firm, "you have the tools." She then turned to look out the window. "But you are having trouble building the house." I should mention here that, above all else, Kelly Troy was a master of metaphor. Any temporary setback was referred to as "a speedbump on the road to the championship"; we were regularly reminded that "there is no elevator to success," but rather, we would be "taking the stairs." I nodded along with Kelly's house-building comment. I could tell I would need to communicate in a way that she could understand. "My house in St. Louis was recently retrofitted for earthquakes," I told her. "And they found a ton of dead rats in the attic," I added.

Kelly pulled a PowerBar out of her desk drawer and offered half to me. I took it, even though it was Strawberry Banana, because I understood that Kelly and I were breaking bread. "Let me put it this way, Ellie," Kelly said, chewing slowly. I took a bite and drooled a little. "The squeaky wheel gets the grease." She went on to explain something that I still think is insane to this day: people who complain more tend to receive more. Simply put, Kelly didn't want to put up with their whining. My eyes now opened, fairness seemed the stuff of childhood dreams.

"I see what you are doing, and I appreciate it," Kelly continued. "Know that." I suddenly felt like an industrious leper quietly performing selfless deeds all for the glory of an all-seeing God in Heaven. What on Earth? I would continue to work hard and keep my head down and be humiliated, meanwhile taking comfort in the fact that Kelly Troy was watching? This didn't sound like much of a deal to me.

I asked her what specific skills she thought I needed to work on, and she said, "All of them." She then pointed out my track and field prowess and told me that running was my strongest asset. This was the best thing about my coach; she mistakenly believed that I was the Missouri State Champion of both the 800-meter run and the mile. I'm not sure why she thought this; our high school relay team had been to the State Championships twice and placed in the Top 8 once, but there was no individual championship on my watch. I had corrected her several times, but by this time, I had given up. "You aren't a drillstopper," Kelly said, taking her second bite of PowerBar. She put the rest of it back in the drawer, and I wondered if she was going to eat anything else that day. According to Kelly, I worked hard and didn't disrupt the other players' productivity, so I could remain on the team. I didn't feel stung by these words; on the contrary, I was surprised to find that I appreciated her honesty.

Four days later, I traveled with the team to a night game at Columbia University. With exactly thirty-eight seconds left on the clock in the first half and a Princeton lead of 18–1 on the scoreboard, Kelly Troy put me in the game as left wing. The adrenaline surged through me, and I leapt off the bench like a bat out of hell. *Rudy . . . Rudy . . . Ellie . . . ELLIE!*

I was terrible, just awful; I missed the one pass that came my way, and even managed to trip on the turf when the play was on the opposite end of the field. It didn't matter; I didn't care. I was on the field. I sat on the bench for the entire second half, but I was so elated that I can barely remember any of it. I never played another minute that season.

I remained on the team for the rest of the year, and through the start of sophomore preseason. A week after our official season had begun, I suspected that history just might repeat itself, and I would not see any playing time that year. One afternoon, after a win against Dartmouth, I approached Kelly at the tailgate. I had made a decision: I told her that I would be leaving the team. Kelly looked at me (or, I think that she did—I couldn't see her eyes in those sunglasses). I believe that I saw a smile dance upon her lips, but it could have just been a twitch. "Ellie, you are going to bloom wherever you are planted," Kelly said. "And I can't give you back the deposit to Barbados." That last part was not a metaphor; the team was to go on a training trip to Barbados that January, and so too, apparently, would my $150 check.

I gave Kelly an uncomfortable hug; her ribs nearly stabbed me, but I didn't care. I was free! I turned to the buffet table to help myself to a second serving of Alyssa Matis's mom's famous apple crisp with vanilla ice cream. I had not met the challenge of excelling—or even being proficient—at college field hockey, but I had accepted this truth. Unexpectedly, I felt at peace with it.

The following week, I auditioned for and was accepted by the campus improvisational comedy group, Quipfire. The week after that, I was sitting around a table at Denny's with the rest of the improv team, this time eating waffles with canned whipped cream. I felt happy. Not only because I was eating yet another delicious confection with dairy topping, but because I had already seen more progress as a new member of this team in a week than I had seen with my former team in a year.

Weirdly, Kelly and I became pretty chummy after I left the field hockey team. When we saw each other around campus, we would smile and wave. I would tell her about my classes; she would tell me about her knee. Like two feuding spouses who decided they might be better off as friends, Kelly and I had reached a new level of understanding. And when it came time for our first Quipfire show, in the middle of October, Kelly Troy was in the front row. It was the first time that she had been to an improv show, and she didn't laugh once. What can I say? Kelly was a stone-cold son of a bitch.

Businesswoman

After my junior year of college, in 2001, two Quipfire teammates and I spent the summer in Chicago. Our improv team had embarked on a tour of the Midwest the previous winter, including three days in Chicago, where we had performed two shows: one at an elementary school and the other at a rich woman's cocktail party. I grew fascinated with the city—not because the rich woman offered to pay us in parsnip-wrapped devils on horseback rather than cash, but because the shows that we saw at the renowned ImprovOlympic and the Second City theatres were simply brilliant. I had laughed so hard I wet my pants, sure, but I had been losing control of my bladder since track meets in high school. No, the new and exhilarating experience here was witnessing the sheer skill with which these improvisers performed. It was like watching a magic show.

iO and Second City had turned out such luminaries as Bill Murray, Mike Myers, Joan Rivers, Amy Sedaris, and, in the years to come, would launch the careers of Steve Carell and Tina Fey. *Maybe you've heard of them?* Frankly put, the city was a goddamned hotbed of comedy and I felt giddy just being there. A small part of me wondered if I, too, could throw my hat in the ring. By now I had been improvising for two years at college, and I had thought about continuing to do comedy after college, but I was too insecure about this idea to admit it. Even to myself, Reader! But now I have just admitted it to you! Anyway, the still far-off notion that I could keep doing comedy after college is exactly what inspired me to join my teammates in Chicago that summer.

At the same time, being a polite teacher's pet from the Midwest, I figured I should also gain experience in a more practical field while I was there. Accordingly, I found one of those incredible opportunities that do not pay money. The advertising internship at Leo Burnett in the copywriting department welcomed me, and I reminded myself how brave I was to allow my parents to cover my housing, food, and improv comedy classes that summer.

My teammates, Scott and Brian, enrolled in the Summer Intensive Course at iO, and I signed up for a Level One class taught by T. J. Jagodowski. T.J. was very famous in the world of improvisers both because he is a genius and also, for reasons unknown to me, he supposedly did not want to work in movies or television. He only wanted to improvise. This made him infinitely more mysterious and also more handsome. The Quipfire alums who then lived in Chicago had given me the scoop on T.J., and they couldn't believe that I had managed to get into a class with him; this would be like taking a painting class with Georgia O'Keeffe, they told me. Actually, I might have told myself that, because I don't know many other painters. Oh, but how I do love Mary Engelbreit!

I was looking forward to working in a more conventional environment during the week, while seeing improv shows and taking classes at night and on the weekends. I would be like a yuppie Jekyll and improviser Hyde, except there would be no serums involved and also no murders (I hoped!). Like a true professional, I knew that I needed a major wardrobe overhaul for my new life as an unpaid businesswoman. I bought three new skirts from Banana Republic (two khaki and one with green flowers), a three-quarter-length sleeved cotton shirt from Talbots, and three white blouses from Ann Taylor. All of my purchases were completed at Plaza Frontenac in St. Louis during the Memorial Day sales, and—when asked if these clothes might be *too* fancy—all saleswomen assured me that these items definitely fell within the parameters of "business casual."

The Leo Burnett summer interns were put up in the Northwestern University residence halls; room rental was $24 per night, plus $150 for an air conditioner. I had my own room with an en suite bathroom, and I said yes to the Huskie Refrigerator Micro-Fridge Unit that was being offered at a substantial summer-only discount. I was delighted to have a spot to store my Philadelphia Cream Cheese Cheesecake Snack Bars, and I found Huskie's claim that it would "transform your room to a micro apartment" to be unequivocally true. Though I had rented a mini-fridge from my own college for the previous three years, microwaves were not allowed in dorm rooms; the idea of heating up and preparing my own food, instead of relying on dining halls or pizza delivery, was intoxicating to me. I walked to and from my internship on Wacker Drive every day, I took the L to ImprovOlympic on Clark Street, and I was responsible for my own meals. It was my first whiff, however faint, of independence. Or, pardon me, was that just the aroma of the Lean Cuisine Café Classics Glazed Chicken warming in my Huskie?

One afternoon, a few weeks into my internship, I was invited to join a creative team working on a radio commercial for the McDonald's Triple Bacon Cheeseburger. I welcomed this opportunity. Up until that point, I had spent a great deal of time pretending to be busy in the cubicle that had been assigned to me.

This was an elaborate act that consisted of moving folders back and forth, shuffling and reshuffling pieces of blank paper while sighing, and writing long letters on yellow legal pads about how bored I was to my sister, Carrie, and my college roommate, Jo. Occasionally, a supervisor would ask me to make photocopies, but most afternoons were devoted to brainstorming sample headlines for *The Onion*: "Dairy Company Introduces Lots-of-Pulp Milk," "Junior High English Student Reads Everything as Metaphor for Acne," "Wife Noticed." I had never heard of *The Onion* before, but there were hard-copy dispensers on every corner in Chicago; I could not believe how incredibly funny it was. Like Sally Hawkins with the creature of water, I seemed to have developed a crush on something that wasn't exactly a person, but was definitely smarter than a fish. I wanted to write headlines so sharp *The Onion* would fall in love with me—have I mentioned that I didn't date much in college? The McDonald's ad arrived as a promising chance to channel this creative energy into work.

Meanwhile, my improv classes were going well. After I received the McDonald's assignment, I felt slightly more confident in class; I wondered if any of my fellow students were as busy a young professional as I was. I knew that Shannon was an attorney, and that David did something with plastics, but beyond that, I might have been the only student juggling both a passion *and* a successful career.

In Quipfire, we mostly performed games; this is known as short-form improv. For example, in a game called Acronym, two improvisers start a scene, and the host interjects periodically with an acronym gathered earlier from the audience. The improvisers then have to form a sentence using words that start with each letter in the acronym; the suggestion "YMCA" might be followed by "You Might Consider A job in the circus!" Hilarious, right?

In T.J.'s class, we were doing longer scenes without as many jokes or punch lines. I found this style to be freeing because it felt closer to how people behaved in real life. T.J. placed great emphasis on simply listening and then responding to our scene partners. While watching shows at night—The Armando Diaz Experience, T.J. and Dave, The Harold—I quickly learned that listening and responding formed the core of Chicago improv. "*Yes, and*" is the first rule of improv anywhere; the idea is that you accept what your scene partner gives you ("*yes*") and add to it without taking anything away ("*and*"). Instructors discouraged stage hogs, and jokes in shows got audible groans. I looked forward to these classes and shows as a soothing respite from my grueling volunteer days at the office—*especially* once I had added the McDonald's gig to my workload.

For the McDonald's assignment, I would shadow a kind-seeming thirty-something copywriter named Jack. We laughed about how his previous account had been Tampax; I asked what that had been like for him, a grown man who doesn't get a period? Philip Morris was also a client of Leo Burnett, and because of this, employees were allowed to smoke indoors. I made some joke about this open smoking policy, then tried to tie in Tampax by pretending to smoke an imaginary tampon, at which point Jack and I both grew quiet.

A couple of days in, Jack told me that I could take a stab at writing copy. I was flattered but felt unqualified; most of the copywriters at Leo Burnett had attended advertising school, and I had no specialized training. "Ellie," Jack said, after I voiced my concerns, "this is a commercial for a *cheeseburger*." His point was not to make it a bigger deal than it was; who couldn't relate to eating a cheeseburger, after all? A vegetarian socialite might have had trouble with this assignment, but I was a meat-eating businesswoman. And so, I rolled up the sleeves of my three-quarter-length-sleeved shirt, making it a short-sleeved shirt, and got to work.

The main idea behind the McDonald's Triple Bacon Cheeseburger was that there was a ton of bacon. In promoting the sandwich to prospective eaters, I was told to really zero in on this feature. I wrote a script that evening in my dorm room, excerpted below:

Sam: Hey, Sue, what's shakin'?
Sue: Nothin' . . . want some bacon?
Sam: Oh, is that what you're makin'?
Sue: Yes, I am makin' bacon.
Sam: Well, for goodness' sakin'!
Sue: Hey, Sam, the leaves need rakin'.
Sam: Well, my back's achin'.
Sue: Are you for real?
Sam: Nah . . . I'm fakin'!

I once heard Stephen King say that ideas flitter and flutter about, and he just hopes to be at his typewriter when one passes over. That's kind of how I felt about my idea to rhyme a lot of words with *bacon*. Genius is sometimes inexplicable, and I consider myself lucky to have been sitting next to my Micro-Fridge with a chewed-up Bic in my hand when this idea floated over me. Otherwise, it would have missed me entirely—bobbing onward past Lou Malnati's Pizzeria, forward to the fields of Grant Park, and then ultimately meeting its death by drowning in the ice-cold waters of Lake Michigan. Phew!

We read our pitches to McDonald's the next day over the phone, and they selected my script. This immediately made me feel both overjoyed and worried. I knew that this was not the correct order of things; we had been learning about status in improv class, and I understood that I had the lower status in my relationship with Jack. I did not mean to embarrass him in front of his colleagues. After all, Jack had a wife and children to feed (or, at least I imagined that he did; as a twenty-one-year-old Catholic, I assumed that all men over the age of thirty were both faithful husbands and dutiful fathers). Who was I to rob him of his manhood, his welfare? I thought of the humiliation he must be feeling and decided to say a prayer for him that night.

In improv scenes, I often played cheerful, optimistic, martyr-like women. These were sort of amped-up versions of myself, and they insisted on seeing the positive side of all events. I summoned this character the next day when I met Jack in his office. While I was always upbeat with him, I figured he would be feeling low after his defeat, and so I decided to bring more than my usual dose of jolliness. "Jack!" I exclaimed when I saw him at his desk. "Your necktie is so beautiful!" Jack smiled and thanked me. Then he handed me a list of actors who were coming to audition for the voiceover that day. I wasn't sure where his sadness was. Instead, it was business as usual as he and I drove to the casting session, selected the "happy, walking bass" music that McDonald's had asked for, and decided which lines to cut from the copy. That evening, as I watched Jack pack up his things and head home to the family he may or may not have had, I gave him a sunny good-bye. "So long, Jack of All Trades!" I called out, using the name "Jack" in a fun way. Jack looked at me, confused. He congratulated me on the radio spot and got on the elevator. I caught my reflection in a glass door and smiled. I was amazing.

One Saturday afternoon in August, a couple of weeks after

the McDonald's recording session had been completed and the commercial had been locked, I was driving with my friend Adam; two years ahead of me at school, he had also been a member of Quipfire and now lived in Chicago as a musician. Scott, Brian, Adam, and I had all just gone to see *A.I.*, that Steven Spielberg movie about a robotic boy who tries to be a human boy. I was trying to figure out how Haley Joel Osment never blinked, and Adam was comparing *A.I.* to a different Spielberg movie that I had never heard of. We passed a KFC, briefly considered going in for some Popcorn Nuggets, and then suddenly, my McDonald's commercial came on the radio. As that old familiar bass line began to play, I gasped and reached for the dial. "That's me!" I told Adam. "This is my commercial!" I had never heard the spot on the actual radio, and I felt like screaming.

"Hey, Sue, is this seat taken?" the radio chattered. "No, Sam, it's vacan . . . t."

Adam laughed out loud. "We love to see you smile," the jingle rang out, and we both whooped uproariously. I was famous! I wondered if I might get discounts at McDonald's for the rest of my life; I wondered if I would have to pay for my hamburgers, at all! Adam and I didn't end up getting any deep-fried Popcorn Nuggets that day, but my feeling of pride was food enough.

When I walked into T.J.'s class the following weekend, I put my head down and avoided eye contact. I was sure that people had been listening to the ad all week, and I didn't want to be hounded by fans. Had my name appeared anywhere in the local radio jingle? No, it had not. Still, I knew that Chicago was a small town—and news like this had a way of traveling quickly.

I sat quietly until it was my turn to do a warm-up scene. T.J. gave us the word *sunset* as a suggestion, and I began staring wistfully out of an imaginary window. "It's nice outside," my scene partner, Peter, said. "We should take a walk before dusk." I turned to look at Peter. "What do you mean?" I snapped. "It's already dark."

The student audience gasped.

T.J. interrupted us then, gently reminding me that I had negated Peter's opening statement. I nodded and apologized. I hadn't even noticed myself doing it. Had fame made me a monster?

That Monday, I was sent with Jack to attend a focus group just outside the city. The *idea* of the Triple Bacon Cheeseburger was a good one, but *what did the people actually think*? We weren't sure, and so we went to find out. But actually, *Jack* went to find out. I just handed out the forms to the focus group attendees and then entered their answers into a computer in the lobby afterward, while Jack hopped on a call with McDonald's. I wasn't sure what was happening. I was a power-hungry advertising executive now. Why was I keyboarding in the lobby?

I casually mentioned this reversal of fortune to Jack on the ride back to Leo Burnett. "Crazy, isn't it," I said, pretending to adjust the air-conditioning. "Writing ads one day, entering data the next." Heat started blasting out of the vents, and I realized I had turned the dial all the way to red. "Not that crazy," Jack pointed out. "You are the intern, after all."

I stared at Jack. The car was quiet. He was right. I was the intern.

But I wanted to be the star.[1]

1 Not really. I did want to keep getting better at improv, though.

Daughter

It was an unusually hot day at the end of May, and my parents had taken the minivan to some other sibling's sports match—I don't know whose. Why would I? As a fourteen-year-old eighth grader about to make her mark in high school the following fall, I needed to focus most of my attention on myself. And yet, even I was not above paying the occasional respect to my own mom and dad. For this reason, I decided that it was worth taking a break from writing my essay on *A Separate Peace* (inside joke for all the *Peace* lovers out there: never sit next to Gene Forrester on a tree branch!) to surprise my dad by washing his car.

His car was already parked in the driveway rather than in the garage; I guess that he had been planning to wash it when he returned home. The truth is, we'll never know what my dad was planning on doing, because—like an overly competitive wise guy jostling a tree branch so that his own friend then falls out of the tree—sometimes certain people take matters into their own hands, and then they ruin other people's Sunday afternoon plans or entire sports careers.

I knew that the S.O.S pads in our own kitchen cleaned our pots and pans to an impeccable shine, so I figured they would do the same for a car. I can hear your objections right now. *You claimed you only play ditzes on television! You seem to think that in real life, you are smart! But what is smart about washing a car with a steel wool soap pad?* Well, I will tell you what is smart about it. On its box, S.O.S tells us that it will make all of our cleaning jobs quicker and easier. Then it boasts that it is versatile enough for cleaning indoors *and out*. Hello! Remember that my father's car was *outside*! But mostly, at the bottom of the box, S.O.S promises to cut through baked-on food, grill residue, *auto grease, and more*. And more! Not only is auto grease mentioned on the box, but it promises to clean even more than that. Anyway, what happened next is not exactly the result of a brilliant mind at work—but it also isn't the result of someone who didn't carefully read the outside of an S.O.S box.

I went outside to wash my dad's car with an S.O.S pad and instead scratched the entire left side of his car with deep streaks that would prove impossible to remove. After the first scratch, I figured that this was simply a gleam from the sun's reflection, and so I kept going. I did notice that the scratches kept happening, but I kept thinking back to the pots and pans. *They just get so shiny*, I thought to myself. *Surely my dad's car will eventually get as shiny as they do*. My dad's car didn't get as shiny as the pots and the pans because the paint was covered in deep, irreparable scratches. When my parents got home and saw the car, their jaws dropped. "What happened?" my mom asked. "Ellie, what did you do?" my dad demanded. I was terrified. "I washed your car with an S.O.S pad," I said slowly. "Only it didn't get as clean as I thought that it would."

My parents looked at me for a minute, curious. What, exactly, had they given birth to? They didn't seem angry. They seemed mostly intrigued. "I can't believe this happened," my dad said. "But there's nothing we can do about it now." I paid for the paint job through a summer's worth of babysitting, but I still don't understand how my parents didn't lose their minds. The truth is, I mess up a lot. And yet my parents never lose faith in me. They probably talk about me when I'm not in the room. But they keep hoping for a stronger tomorrow.

However, they are not my only parents. I am also the daughter of several fictional TV parents. Sometimes I get confused about exactly *whose* daughter I am. I generally do a pretty good job of separating my personal life from my professional life. Occasionally, though, I get so deep into the role of Daughter that I forget who I am. Here are some of the people who have played my parents:

1) Joan Cusack

In the series finale of *The Office*, Erin is reunited with her birth parents. I apologize if I just spoiled anything for any viewers who haven't reached that point yet, but it's 2018 and the finale was five years ago! Erin's father was played by Ed Begley Jr., and her mother by Joan Cusack. On our last day of shooting, I was saying good-bye to Joan Cusack in the parking lot, and I happened to mention how much I liked her cardigan. There was nothing splashy about the cardigan, nor was there anything that unusual. It was just a beautiful, comfortable, marigold-yellow piece, and I liked it. Can you even guess what Joan Cusack did next? She took the cardigan right off and gave it to me. "Oh, no!" I protested. "That's too much!" Joan Cusack looked me in the eye and told me how very much she wanted me to take her cardigan. "I had such a nice time here," she said, gesturing to the parking lot. Even in my heightened emotional state, I understood that she was referring to her experience on *The Office* and not that specific parking lot. "I would love to give this to you as a token of my appreciation!" Joan Cusack wasn't trying to make a scene; she was just a well-raised woman who must have had some extra cardigans lying around at home. I accepted her gift, and I have never worn it. I am too scared that I might get it dirty. So, I just keep it next to a clear box in my closet marked "Winter Clothes" in a different clear box, marked "Joan Cusack's Clothes."

2) Ed Begley Jr.

Another parent I have is the man who played Erin's biological father. Ed Begley Jr. has acted in more than 310 different projects, and, at the time we shot *The Office* finale, I had acted in almost eight. One of my projects had been an independent movie called *Cayman Went*, about a fading Hollywood underwater action star who visits, and then leaves, the Cayman Islands—so I figured there was no need for me to feel intimidated by the chops of my fellow actor.

There is a very moving part of the reunion scene between Erin and her parents, and it happens when they embrace. It is so sweet. Erin's parents had been in the audience at a panel about the documentary, and they reveal themselves while Erin is on stage. As I would run down to meet them, Ed Begley Jr. would start to cry. And I don't mean some gentle sniffles. I mean some intense, committed, heartfelt sobs. I couldn't believe it. *How can this guy cry so many times?* I kept thinking to myself. *It's like he doesn't want to stop!* I was so jealous. I can never make myself cry on camera! Here are the tricks that I have tried, and they have all proved useless:

- Thinking of people I know who have died.
- Thinking of people I am mad at.
- Holding my breath and trying to force the blood to my face so that my eyes water.
- Opening my eyes really wide and not blinking.
- Thinking of more people I know who have died.
- Thinking of our environment.
- Yawning twenty times in a row.
- Remembering the acting lesson that Megan Draper gives Sally Draper, in which she teaches her how to cry on cue.
- Focusing on what is happening to my character in the scene.
- Thinking of people I don't even know who have died.

What usually happens with me is that some poor makeup artist is forced to come up to my face and blow in my eyes through a tear straw, which is a glass tube filled with menthol crystals. This makes my eyes water right away, and then my brain gets mixed up, and starts to think that I really *am* sad. If this happens, sometimes I do actually begin to cry on my own! Anyway, I don't do drugs, so having menthol blown through a straw in my face feels wild.

The point is, Ed Begley Jr. is a phenomenal actor, and I really hope he never caught my beautiful makeup artist, Dionne, blowing menthol in my eyes offstage.

3) Lisa Kudrow

Why do I keep getting cast as naïve women who were separated from their parents at a young age? As Kimmy on *Unbreakable Kimmy Schmidt*, I am also reunited with my birth mother—but this birth mother is played by Lisa Kudrow. What is it like having Lisa Kudrow as a mom? It is a cross between loving *Friends* and being obsessed with *The Comeback*. That lady is amazing.

When we filmed the episode of *Kimmy* starring Lisa Kudrow, I was about eight weeks' pregnant. According to my doctor, the fetus was the size of a raspberry. I love raspberries and was delighted to think about my little baby as being a little raspberry! But I was also supposed to ride a roller coaster as Kimmy. In the episode, Kimmy learns that her birth mother is a self-proclaimed "coasterhead" and so Kimmy heads to Universal Studios, determined not only to find her, but also to promote as much corporate synergy as she can (*Kimmy* streams on Netflix and is produced by NBC Universal). Kimmy does find her mom, and the two of them proceed to have an enormous fight on a gigantic roller coaster. Since my recently acquired maternal instinct told me that it would not be a good idea for a pregnant person to be on a roller coaster—even if her baby was just the size of a small berry—I told Tina Fey, the co-creator of our show, about my pregnancy, and she immediately said there was no way I was going on a roller coaster. This put the kibosh on the whole idea, and we did the roller coaster scenes on a green screen instead.

However, even though the effects of steep drops and suspenseful climbs would be achieved through the work of green screen magic, we would still film the beginning of the roller coaster scenes on an actual roller coaster. This was terrifying, because it was never clear to us if the car would stop before it began to climb the first hill. Lisa Kudrow and I would get into the car and lower our over-the-shoulder restraints. The detail to keep in mind here is that these restraints *did not lock*; they were simply placed over our shoulders. The car would begin to advance. We would say our lines, me first, then her, and then the car was supposed to stop. But here is the thing. The car rarely stopped until *just* before it began to climb. Every take was a Russian roulette, and my body was pure adrenaline. And yet Lisa Kudrow did not bat an eye. "I wonder why they don't stop it sooner," she murmured to me after the fourth or fifth take. "It's a little scary." This woman taught me calmness in the face of potential roller coaster death.

4) An ethereal middle-aged woman with low bone density.

Almost a decade ago, I played an easygoing woman on a breezy beach whose silver-haired mother urged her to take Caltrate. This product is a calcium supplement, and my on-screen mother confided in me some of her deepest secrets. "[My own] mom knew I needed calcium from Day One. Now I'm the mom," she told me. She knew that 80 percent of us don't get enough calcium from food. And then, she leaned in close for the ugly reality of the situation: *"Our bodies can steal calcium from our bones!"* I knew that my mom was sharing with me some very personal details that only a daughter should know, and I felt close to her after our talk. *My mom might have naturally weak bones*, I thought to myself at the time. *But she makes up in*

> *wisdom what she lacks in calcium deposits.* I learned a lot from that particular mother, and not all of it was calcium-related. Some of it was about how to appear natural while moving the hair that has gotten blown into your sticky lip gloss thanks to high winds on the beach.

My real-life parents possess the selflessness of Joan Cusack, the empathy of Ed Begley Jr., the fearlessness of Lisa Kudrow, and the enviable calcium levels of my Caltrate mom.

And I am very lucky to be their daughter.

Improviser

After college graduation, I wasn't sure what to do next. It felt too late in the game to try medicine, but still too early to retire. A career in education seemed appealing, but I couldn't shake the little voice that kept reminding me how kids could be twerps. Comedy was still a possibility, though a remote one. I didn't know many professional comedians personally, and the ones I did know were older friends from college who held day jobs as well; the odds of being able to make comedy a full-time profession, to me, seemed low. And so, I decided to put off making any enormous, adult decisions by continuing to go to school. *Education is a journey*, I told myself. *Plus, your parents can probably be persuaded to spring for your tuition and then you won't need to make any big moves for a year.*

And so I spent nine months in England, where I studied British literature at Oxford. My focus was nineteenth-century British fiction, but most of my energy went into the Oxford University Dramatic Society (OUDS) and McVitie's Digestives. These scrumptious biscuits made me feel healthy because of the word *digestive*, but really, they are just cookies—and the very best ones have chocolate and caramel on top. Anyway, having all of these new English cookies at my disposal was invigorating—and I enjoyed being involved with OUDS, even starring in the chorus of *My Fair Lady* at Magdalen College that spring—but I felt impatient to get back home. I knew that I didn't want to pursue academics at a professional level, and I wasn't quite sure what I was doing there, besides eating all the McVitie's.

Then, the following summer, I performed in a children's play at the Edinburgh Fringe Festival. The play was called *The White Slipper*, and mostly what I remember is a lot of ribbon work. However, spending three weeks in Edinburgh and seeing a ton of comedy reminded me how much I missed doing improv. I saw Baby Wants Candy, a Chicago improv-musical group, more than a dozen times. I saw Jo Brand's stand-up act twice. I saw the Flight of the Conchords do their show *High on Folk*, I caught Demetri Martin in his one-man show *If I*, and I watched Waen Shepherd perform his character Gary Le Strange. These live performances electrified me: is it too bold to say that I suddenly felt that I, too, might be able to do something like that? *Because I did.* I guess that sometimes it just takes a year of having no real direction or consistent sunlight for the fiery heart to let its passions be known. As it turned out, my own fiery heart was dying to go for the laughs.

My Quipfire friend Scott had just graduated from college the previous spring, and he also wanted to pursue comedy. Another Quipfire friend, Tommy Dewey, had moved to New York after graduating a couple of years earlier, and proceeded to book commercial work within a year. He then moved to Los Angeles, but his success in New York was encouraging to Scott and me. We didn't consider going to LA—there were too many other aspiring actors there!—and though we knew Chicago was the capital of improv, it seemed like New York might afford us more opportunities for television and commercial work. Honestly, though, why did we think we knew anything? Scott was twenty-two, I was twenty-three, and neither of us had been on any kind of audition outside of school theatre. But as Quipfire alums and good friends, we shared the vague notion that we would enroll in improv classes in New York and try to put on shows together.

We found an apartment on Eightieth Street across from Zabar's on the Upper West Side. The next piece of business was to sign up for a Level One improv class at the Upright Citizens Brigade (UCB). This theatre was founded by UCB troupe members Matt Besser, Amy Poehler, Ian Roberts, and Matt Walsh; they had been trained at ImprovOlympic in Chicago, written and starred in their own sketch show on Comedy Central, and opened their first theatre in Manhattan in 2000. To any aspiring New York improviser, this place was a dream. In order to perform on a house team there, a student had to complete all five levels of the curriculum. Feeling like I had no time to waste, I decided to take classes back to back with no break in between. It would still take me a full year to finish. (The only reason I could even consider doing it that way was that I was in the rare position of being able to reach out to my parents for money if I needed it.)

And yet not even Daddy could save me from vermin. A recent perusal of some emails exchanged between Scott, Brian Kerr (our third roommate), and me reveals some harsh truths:

On Wednesday, January 21, 2004 10:21AM, Scott Eckert wrote:

> I killed a roach today when it fell out of the dishes cabinet. (Sorry I bent up your old Newsweek, Ellie.) . . .

BE CAREFUL!

-Scott

Am I reproducing this email to brag that I used to read *Newsweek*? A little. But mostly I am showing you that our apartment was gross.

On Friday, 18 June 2004 11:15:58 -0700 (PDT), Ellie Kemper wrote:

i just emptied out the trash from the sink and after i removed the trashbag from the can there were a dozen writhing maggots or mealworms on the bottom. it has repulsed me to the core and i feel ill.

On Friday, June 18, 2004 2:26 PM, Brian Kerr wrote:

what type of food? who leaves meat out? me? eeeeeeeeew
Is this the regular trash bag?
eeeeeeeeeeew

Why does Brian bother to ask what type of food was left out? All types of food! Don't leave any of it out!

One afternoon I walked into our apartment to find Scott eating a lunch that was completely orange: three slices of cheddar cheese, a handful of carrots, and a large helping of Doritos. Scott looked up at me helplessly from the couch. "What are we doing?"

He was asking the wrong person. My only standing appointment was going to watch Asssscat at UCB every Sunday night. The later show, at 9:30, was free, but sometimes I had trouble staying up that late. So I usually paid the $5 to go see the 7:30 show. Amy Poehler performed most Sundays, and Horatio Sanz did, too. This was certainly the highlight of my week, though I once opened my At-A-Glance weekly calendar and, seeing "Asssscat–7:30" under Sunday as the only event written, began to sob. *What is your life, Ellie?* I said out loud while also watching myself in the mirror to see how I looked when I cried. *What is the plan here?*

In retrospect, I see that I did, in fact, have a plan. My younger, weeping self just loved a little melodrama, is all. My plan was to enroll in improv classes at the Peoples Improv Theater (PIT) and UCB. I would perform improv shows with Scott wherever I could. After I had completed my classes, I would audition to be on a house team at both theatres. While I was doing all of that, I would work on my writing. I would submit to free publications and try to figure out how to contribute to *The Onion.* My sister had interned at *Late Night with Conan O'Brien* the previous summer, and maybe I would try to get an internship there as well. As a twenty-three-year-old, I loved nothing more than a big fat cry in the pillows, but as someone who is ~~wiser and~~ older now, I see that I did have several concrete goals.

Therefore, despite the maggots and roaches and orange lunches staring me down at every turn, I was able to carry on. Scott and I completed our Level One class at UCB, and we had also started taking an Intro class at the PIT. We were taught to listen to our scene partners and to build scenes as a team. Showboats were discouraged and class clowns frowned upon, which a UCB classmate of mine found out when he decided to squeeze his testicles through his open fly as he entered a scene one afternoon. "Tim," our teacher said, turning away from his student's balls. "Don't do that."

The reason I fell in love with improv in the first place was the simple concept of listening and responding, so I felt relieved that both theatres embraced this tenet. Moreover, the improv structure at both places was long form. As opposed to the short-form games we had played in college, long-form scenes took what I loved most about improv—truthful reaction in the moment, building on what your scene partner has set forth, creating the scene as an ensemble—and fleshed it out even more. One of my very favorite scenes in college had been during a rare long-form piece; Tommy Dewey played a typewriter-pounding Angela Lansbury witnessing a murder that Scott committed in a cigar lounge. It is precisely this sort of delightfully unexpected turn of events, discovered by performers and audience alike in real time, that makes me adore improv.

After Scott and I completed our Intro level at the PIT, we started performing in a weekly Wednesday night show called "The Mosh," where any improviser could show up and play. We met a bunch of other improvisers through "The Mosh," and in the spring of 2004, Scott, Chris Caniglia, Tom Ridgely, Megan Martin, Justin Akin, Dave Lombard, Kristen Schaal, and I formed a team. Against my really strong protests, we named ourselves Big Black Car. I hated this name and I still do. It is the name of a song by Gregory Alan Isakov, which makes it even worse. But though I hated the name of this team, I loved the team itself. We started booking shows in comedy venues around the city—Juvie Hall, Parkside Lounge, Rififi, Under St. Mark's—and we rehearsed as often as we could. (Many people don't understand how you can rehearse improvisation, but there are countless forms that improv groups experiment with—my favorite form with Big

Black Car was called the Big Black Ballet, which incorporated dance edits into the show—and even though you are making up the show as you go along, the ability to do that requires practice. Also, listening carefully is a skill set just like any other. Hear that, MEN? I'm kidding.[1])

Separately, Scott and I started performing two-person improv shows at the PIT that summer. We called our show "At the End of the Day," and it was a long-form show with no games or rigid structure. We basically did several five-minute scenes, then circled back to revisit the characters established in those scenes; sometimes characters from different scenes met each other, and we always tried to wrap up the stories of these characters as best we could in the final scene. We were also working on a written sketch show so that we would have something to submit to comedy festivals; its working title was "Hope Be Gone."

Meanwhile, I had completed all five levels of classes at UCB, which meant that I was now eligible to audition for a Harold team. "Harold" was the form of improv that these teams performed at shows; a Harold consists of three chapters of three scenes, punctuated by two group games in between chapters. Auditions were held on a Saturday afternoon in November, and I received an email the next day informing me I had gotten a callback! I was excited but cautious. I called my mom and dad and delivered the good news; they were predictably happy for me, but my mom warned me not to be disappointed if they gave the spot to someone who had been there longer and thus had paid more of her dues. That Monday evening at callbacks, I per-

1 Not kidding at all. Men, try to listen better!

formed in three two-person scenes and a group game, and I left feeling like I had done my best.

On Tuesday, November 23, I received this email. I was so happy that I didn't even care about Owen leaving the second "e" off my name!!!

> From Owen Burke
>
> 11/23/04 at 12:25 PM
>
> Congratulations!
>
> you did it up!
>
> Eric Appel
>
> Elli Kemper
>
> Kristy Kershaw
>
> Rachel Korowitz
>
> Matt Moses
>
> Shannon O'Neill
>
> Gavin Speiller
>
> Dave Thunder
>
> . . . now get together, find a coach and start rehearsing. Your first show is in December.
>
> Contact me for anything.
>
> Total Respect,
>
> Owen

Our team finally decided on the name Mailer Daemon (other contenders were Easy Lover, Brokaw, The Dream Police, and Gigantor), and we began rehearsing right away. By the winter of 2005, I was performing on Tuesdays with Mailer Daemon at UCB and Wednesdays with Big Black Car at the

PIT. Scott and I had been given the 9:30 p.m. Saturday slot at the PIT for "At the End of the Day." I was getting so good at improv it almost wasn't funny. *Is this how Elaine May feels?* I asked myself on more than one occasion, referring to one of the greatest improvisers of all time. *No*, a voice called back to me. *She is a genius, a living legend. You do not feel how Elaine May feels.*

Being a member of these teams and performing in these shows felt like measurable progress. Now when my parents' friends asked me what projects I was working on, I could say that I was an improviser at two theatres with weekly shows in Manhattan. Ha! Furthermore, my friend Ptolemy Slocum had told his commercial agent Maura Maloney to come see one of Big Black Car's shows that winter. She enjoyed the show and invited me to come to her agency, CESD, to meet with some of the other agents there. I signed with their commercial agency the following week and booked two commercials the week after that: one for DSW (Designer Shoe Warehouse) and one for Aquafina. Suddenly I was a working actor!

Scott and I finished writing "Hope Be Gone" in the summer of 2005, and we submitted it to UCB. We wanted to get a run at the theatre to bring in theatrical agents, producers, and other executives in showbiz. Anthony King, who was the artistic director at UCB at that time, liked our show but had some ideas for where it could be improved. He also suggested changing the title of our show, and we all agreed that "Death and/or Despair" would be the winner. After implementing Anthony's notes and working with our friend Jen Nails as well, we received a run at the UCB in October of 2005. Here was our postcard:

The show was all about sadness. It consisted of six segments, including a 1930s-style newsroom romance and a wordless portrait of a heartbroken woman set to Natalie Merchant's "My Skin." But what really captured the essence of our show was its opening dance, set to the Disney World soundtrack "Epcot Illusions":

> Lights up on Ellie, alone reading a magazine. Sound of footsteps approaching, faster and faster. Scott appears from backstage. Intense chase sequence ensues. Audience follows as Scott chases Ellie down a fireman's pole, riding stallions, digging holes, snorkeling under water, dueling with swords, grocery cart shopping, and an ultimate, decisive game of

chess. Ellie wins. Scott slashes Ellie's throat. Ellie falls to ground, dead. Scott licks bloody knife in victory.

Scott and I received a run of our show at the UCB for November and December 2005. Anthony had also submitted our show to the HBO Aspen Comedy Festival. We were ecstatic because this festival was *the* place for aspiring comedians to make their mark. We did not receive a callback, so our ecstasy quickly gave way to agony. But then our agony gave way to excitement because we still had a two-month run at UCB, and we were packing the house!

On the job side of things, I was lucky to be enjoying a steady string of commercial work. Though my DSW and Aquafina ads only aired locally, I booked a bunch of jobs—Kmart, Wendy's, M&Ms, Cingular, Citibank—that went national. This was great, because an actor is paid based on the number of times the spot airs, and making money through commercials allowed me greater independence and more time to work on writing and putting up shows. While I continued to perform with Big Black Car and my Harold team (which had undergone a reshuffle in the meantime, losing some members and adding others—we were now called "fwand"), I also started writing more. I began contributing to *McSweeney's* regularly (my first piece, "Listen, Kid, The Biggest Thing You've Got Going for You Is Your Rack," had been accepted in December 2005), and I finally was invited to contribute headlines to *The Onion* around the same time. I had persistently badgered Joe Garden, the features editor, for a solid year—me sending him headline after headline, him suggesting improvement after improvement—until finally he added me to the group of contributing writers. I did not know Joe Garden previously or have any connection to him; I saw his name on the masthead and mailed a hard copy letter to *The Onion* office addressed to him. I had picked him because he was listed first alphabetically. Luckily, I happened to pick one of the friendliest and most generous people I have ever had the pleasure of knowing.

I also started working on a one-person show. I called this show *Dumb Girls*, and it was a character showcase of ladies who weren't too bright. I put it up at UCB in the fall of 2006, and it got some good attention, but nothing Earth-shattering.

I went back to work on a different one-person show that I would eventually call *Feeling Sad/Mad with Ellie Kemper*. This was a show about ladies whose lives were falling apart. Writing this show felt like torture, because I wasn't sure what I was trying to do. Everything that I came up with felt clichéd, and I found that I, too, was beginning to feel pretty sad and mad myself! Thankfully, I enlisted the help of Jason Mantzoukas, a friend from UCB, and he whipped the show into shape. We created a manic airline attendant "host," who would serve as the through line. We gradually developed five other crazy ladies, and the premise of the show was that these ladies were all waiting at various spots in the airport for their Alaska Airlines Flight #404 to board. And then the airplane crashes before it even gets to the airport. It took a lot of performances to get this show right. One night, I performed to a mostly full house and—no exaggeration—there was *one laugh*. I wanted to die. In fact, walking to the subway after that show, I vowed to quit comedy. By the time I emerged from the subway, however, I had decided to rejoin comedy. I went into my apartment, put on a DVD of *The Tracey Ullman Show*, realized that I would never be as talented as Tracey Ullman, but that I would still like to be a performer.

That brief surge of adrenaline that I'd felt when improvising in *Christmas Magic* so many years ago had managed to carry me through the next decade and a half. The truth is, I enjoyed the exhilaration and the thrill of not knowing what was coming next. I am also a fairly obedient person in real life, so it's therapeutic to play women who are slightly unhinged on stage.

I received a run of *Sad/Mad* at UCB in the summer of 2008, and in August, I was invited to perform in a showcase for *Saturday Night Live* (more on this juicy nugget later). The *SNL* audition brought me to the attention of other showrunners and agents. And *that* is why I was able to get a meeting with Greg Daniels and Mike Schur from *The Office* in the fall of 2008. But none of that would have taken place if I had not written a show for myself, created characters to perform, and made a product to share with the industry.

Also: luck. So much of show business comes down to good luck. And if you have it, be sure to sprinkle it on others. That's what she said? Keep reading . . .

Hysteric

A lot of people with whom I email seem not to share my love of exclamation points. Or all caps. Or my fervent devotion to the sign-off "Best." Does this make our communication a tad more difficult? Well, yeah. As someone who is frightened of anyone else not being positively delighted at all times, I live in a near-constant state of fear that I have accidentally offended the person with whom I am communicating. *Why did she only use a period when advising me to have a good day?*

The complaints about my emails are always the same: "You write back really quickly," "You don't give me enough time to respond," "You sure do use a lot of exclamation points!" But the complaint I get the most—the one that, if it were a singer on *American Idol*, and complaints were votes, would become our next American Idol—is this: "It makes me anxious to read your AHAHAHAHHAHAHAHAHAHHAHAHAHHAHAAA's when you think that something is funny. Why don't you just use 'lol'?"

And suddenly, I don't care so much about these people feeling positively delighted.

I am so sorry, glum email correspondents everywhere. I didn't realize that email was such an elegant and fancy form of communication. I didn't realize that it was too "refined" for raw or unchecked emotion. I didn't realize that I had to write my emails *with a freaking quill.*

AHAHAHHHAHAHAHAHHAAA

HAHHAHAHAHAHHAHAA

AHAHAHAHAHHAHAHAHAHHAHAHAHAHAH-HAHAHHAAAAA

In college, I took a class on poetry. And do you know what I learned in that class? That I don't understand what's so great about "The Tyger." Do you know what else I learned in that class? That one of my classmates had written a very long word in his notebook: *onomatopoeia*. Curious and confused and consumed with a quenchless thirst for copying my classmates' notes, I wrote this funny word down in my own notebook.

Fifteen years later, while hiding in my parents' basement so I wouldn't have to help clean up after Thanksgiving dinner, I found this college poetry notebook. I was way too busy to take the time to look through it at that moment, but when I came back for Christmas three weeks after that, I saw this word, *onomatopoeia*, still written down in my cute college handwriting. I decided to look it up. And do you know what I learned? That my parents had lost their dictionary one night in a game of Fictionary that had gotten out of control—and that they hadn't even bothered to buy a new one. "Typical Dotty and David Kemper," I said to myself out loud.

Not ready to give up just yet, I turned on my iPhone and I googled "onomatopoeia definition." My dumb phone kept typing *m* when I needed *n*, and then reminded me that I hadn't backed up my phone in seventy-four weeks. "I hate this phone!" I shouted passionately in the basement. Eventually my phone got the word spelled correctly, and I was able to get on with my day.

Onomatopoeia means: the creation of words that imitate natural sounds. And *onomatopoeia* is pronounced: ON-O-MA-TO-PEE-UH. If that's not a great word for a game with words, I don't know what is!

The point to take away from all of this research is: if AHAHAHHAHAHAHAHHAHAAA isn't a word imitating the most natural sound in the whole world, then I wouldn't want to be right.

Here's the thing about "lol": What? What in the hell does that even mean? That I'm Laughing Out Loud? Yeah, that really comes across when I'm reading it. *Hmph*, I think to myself, sounding out the words of your email. *Michelle wrote "lol"—she must be laughing really, REALLY hard right now. The intensity of this laughter is just LEAPING off the page. I get it! I really get it!! "Lol," man—"lol" forever!*

Did I mention that I am being sarcastic? Because I am, you filthy animal. I REALLY AM!

SO SUE ME FOR ENJOYING A LITTLE BIT OF FEELING IN THIS WORLD!!!!!

Here is what I think of the complaint about AHAHAHHAHAHAAAA: [I just pretended to throw up.] Excuse me, but do you think that I am doing this for my own pleasure? Do you think that I am sitting here, and that I am reading what you wrote, and that I am *choosing* to burst out with some of the most uncontrollable laughter that I have ever known? Do you think that I am *enjoying* this monstrous *roar* clawing itself out of me, consuming my every fiber, ruling over my every nerve? Do you think that this is somehow *fun for me*?

AHAHAHHAHAHAHAHAAAAAAHAHHAHAHAAA

Do you think that I don't *wish* that "lol" could adequately express how hard I am laughing, but that using "lol" would be like using "splash" for the uncontainable RAAAAAAAAARR-RRGGGHHHH that is Niagara Falls?

Do you think that I am a freaking piece of WOOD?

I guess what I have to ask you here is this: what exactly are you so afraid of? Or maybe this is the better question: what exactly are you running away from? Because in my SoulCycle class, I am told to run *toward* the fear, not *away* from it, and so if I knew what your own fear *was*, I could probably run *toward* it and then *punch it in the face for you*.

And oh, how we would all laugh about it then!!!!!!!!!!!!!!!

Look, I'm not here to beg and plead and moan for you to keep emailing me. I'm really not. Life is too short for tears, man—and too long not to laugh. So, thank you for the emails, and I'll see you on the other side.

AHAHHAHAHAHHAHAAAAA

no, my friend

I'll SEE YOU IN HELL

HAHHAHAHAHAAHHHHAHHAHAHAHAA

DO YOU HEAR ME?!

I WILL SEE YOU IN HELL!!!!!!!!!!!!!!!!

AHAHAHHAHAHAHAAA

HAHAHHAHAHAHHAHAHAHHAHAHHAHHA-HAHAHHAHAHHAHAAAAAAA

Best,

Ellie

Actress

I will never forget where I was the first time I asked a middle-aged man sitting next to me whether *lien* was pronounced "lee-EN" or "lean." I guess nobody could forget a thing like that.

"It's lean," he said.

"I know in French, it would be 'lee-EN,'" I went on. "I took French in high school." For some reason, he didn't seem impressed.

"I have a mortgage," he told me. "And it's pronounced 'lean.'"

We were in midtown Manhattan at a commercial audition for a mortgage company, and you could have cut the tension in that waiting room with a radial arm saw. My line was "That's news to me. Are you sure?" Then I must have said something about a lien, but I don't recall exactly what. All I remember is that I needed to know how to pronounce it, and fast.

But the reason I remember that audition so clearly has nothing to do with home loans or the increased foreclosure rates that had already led to a subprime mortgage crisis that steamy summer of 2008. The reason is that as I was leaving the building (I had gone with my French pronunciation, "lee-EN," and was promptly corrected by the director), I checked my voicemail. I had a message from my manager telling me that Lorne Michaels wanted to meet with me at 5:00.

What?!

A couple of nights earlier, I had performed in a comedy showcase at the Upright Citizens Brigade Theatre in Chelsea. While not advertised as such, the showcase was essentially a first-round audition for *Saturday Night Live*; Lorne Michaels and several producers from the show had been in the audience.

And now Lorne Michaels wanted to meet with me at 5:00!

I immediately panicked. Should I go home to shower first? I had just come out of the audition, so I already had clean hair and some tinted Chapstick on. How much fancier could I get? I wasn't sure—but I raced home anyway and then decided there was no time to shower. I called my manager. "Why are you still at your apartment?" he cried. "You need to be at 30 Rock in an hour!"

I ran out of my apartment!

I sprinted to the subway station at Seventy-Second Street. I wanted to feel like Mary Tyler Moore! I knew that she threw her hat in the air, but I didn't have a hat!

I made a conscious decision to forget about the hat, and instead I boarded the 1 train. When I emerged from underground at Fiftieth and Broadway, I took a deep, focused breath. I knew that I needed to quiet my mind; lucky for me, there is no place to quiet your mind like the northernmost edges of Manhattan's Times Square. Memories from the UCB show came flooding over me, and I allowed myself to sit in the waters of reminiscence for a moment—but not long enough to get pruney.

The performance two evenings earlier had been broken into two parts. The first part was a character showcase; each comedian had about five minutes to present whatever character he or she chose. I had chosen Marie-Christine, a Parisian teenager whose dog had recently drowned in the Seine. The second part was an improvisation panel moderated by the artistic director, Anthony King. We all sat in a row of chairs onstage, each playing a new character while Anthony asked us all sorts of nonsense questions.

For the panel, I had played a character who was a combination of a former teacher of mine and a piece that I had written for *McSweeney's*. This former teacher—whom I will not name, because I want all of my former teachers to try to guess which one it is. What a fun game for the former teachers!—is a delightful woman with unwavering optimism. The *McSweeney's* character grew out of a piece I wrote called "A Guest Columnist Still Getting the Hang of It." This guest columnist can, both fortunately and unfortunately, see all sides of every issue, and has trouble deciding on a firm stance. I thought this would be a good choice for a character panel because the game of vacillating between opposite opinions while being relentlessly cheerful felt like a nice challenge and—more important, given the circumstances—something that I could pull off.

The other people in the showcase were Charlie Sanders, Eugene Cordero, Nate Lang, Aubrey Plaza, Jeff Hiller, Sue Galloway, and Kate McKinnon. I knew all of these crazy cats from the theatre, though I have not received their official blessing to refer to them in this paragraph as "crazy cats." Nonetheless, being with these crazy cats was the best part of the night. Hanging out in the greenroom beforehand wasn't stress-filled; it was *fun*. Obviously, I felt nervous, but I was mostly just excited. It felt like an amped-up UCB show with friends, and not an audition at all.

(Of course, it *was* an audition, arguably the most important audition of my life, and I needed to ace it.)

I left the theatre that night on a high. The audience had been enthusiastic and on our side the entire time. I felt satisfied because I had gotten laughs, and I felt pleased because I would not have done anything differently. As the great Kelly Troy would have said, I had left everything on the field.

I must have been smiling to myself during this reverie, because back in Midtown, a drunk businessman was asking me "what in heaven's hell [was I] so happy about." I looked at that drunk businessman, gave him a huge grin, and I told him I was on my way to the meeting of a lifetime. Then I started running because what if the drunk businessman was an angry drunk?

I entered the Forty-Ninth Street entrance of 30 Rock as instructed and handed my ID to security. I immediately began trying to win over the guard, very aware of the possibility that he might be good friends with Lorne Michaels. "I sure was tired that day," I told the guard, pointing to my driver's license photo. "Probably hungover." I laughed and leaned in close. "Remember those days?" I leaned back out and waved my hands in the air. "You know I do!" I yelled. The guard gave me my temporary badge and pointed toward the elevators. I could tell he would rave about me to Lorne Michaels.

I rode the elevator to the eighth floor of Rockefeller Plaza. A place I never, not in a million years, could have imagined I might visit in a non-tour capacity. Yes, I had interned at *Late Night with Conan O'Brien* for six months in 2005, but that studio was on the sixth floor. The eighth floor was two floors up—but a million miles away! The elevator doors parted, and I checked in with a page sitting at a desk. "I'm Ellie Kemper and I'm here to meet Michael Lornes," I heard myself saying.

The page giggled, and I corrected myself. "The name you have on your list might be 'Elizabeth,' not 'Ellie,'" I added. "That's my legal name. It's also my confirmation name." The page told me that she had "Ellie" on her list, and that she would escort me to Lorne Michaels's office. I realized then that I had said Lorne Michaels's name wrong; I thought about throwing myself out the window right then and there but decided that a crash would make a bigger scene than any rumor about mixing up Lorne Michaels's name. So I kept walking. I sat down in a small antechamber, and the page asked if I wanted any coffee or water. I knew that she was testing my stamina, and so I told her I needed nothing. She nodded and left, and I sat in that chair—very still, and very thirsty—for the following two or maybe three hours.

Over those hours, several people on the *SNL* staff popped in to introduce themselves, and all of those people seemed nice. Still, I felt as though I might throw up at any minute. This was an enormous moment in my life, a high-pressure situation for which I had had zero time to prepare. Furthermore, unlike many of my comedy friends, I did not possess an encyclopedic knowledge of the history of *SNL*; this was causing me a large amount of anxiety. As a teenager, I had watched the show most weekends, but I had been just as interested in doing well on my SATs, passing my driver's test, and racking up more community service hours than anyone else in my class so that I could, once and for all, establish myself as the most benevolent student at our school. Lorne Michaels and *Saturday Night Live* were from a universe that was not quite my own. I was Aladdin at Princess Jasmine's palace—a street urchin in the midst of royalty, I had no business being here!

At last, a young woman entered the waiting area and invited me into Lorne Michaels's office. The smell of hot popcorn beckoned me, and I fell into step behind this lady. She opened the door, and there, behind a regular-sized desk, sat Lorne Michaels. And there, also behind that desk but slightly to the right of it, sat Seth Meyers! This calmed me down immediately. I had seen Seth Meyers perform at the UCB in Asssscat, and he seemed both kind and normal. Kind and normal people put me at ease, and I could feel my heart rate drop ever so slightly.

I took a seat in the chair opposite these two men and folded my hands. Lorne Michaels[1] introduced himself and thanked me for coming. Then he asked in which part of the city I lived. It turned out that we both lived on the Upper West Side, and Lorne Michaels mentioned a great bodega on Seventy-Fourth Street. I told him I would definitely have to try it.

After that, he asked me if I was trying to be an actress. I knew in that moment I was a goner. How on Earth was I supposed to answer this question? If I said, "No, sir. I already *am* an actress," then would I sound delusional? Other than several commercials, I had no acting credits to my name. Lorne Michaels personally knew Tom Hanks and Nicole Kidman—real actors and actresses who went to parties in the Hollywood Hills! On the other hand, if I got on *SNL*, wouldn't Lorne Michaels want credit for turning me *into* an actress? There was no right answer; there were only more traps. So, I said, "Yeah!"

Lorne Michaels seemed satisfied with this answer.

1 You will notice that I keep referring to Lorne Michaels by both his first and last name. That's because certain people—Tina Fey, Steve Carell, Michelle Obama—should be called by both their first and last names (unless you are family, spouse, or personal surgeon).

There is only one other part of the conversation that I remember. Lorne Michaels asked me "what era of the show" I had grown up on. I smiled. My mind was all white curtains and pillows. I could think of nothing. I had watched *Saturday Night Live* at Emily Sinclair's house most Saturdays because her parents hadn't seemed to mind if we stayed up late, but I found that I could not remember any human words in this moment at 30 Rock. I don't mean that I couldn't just remember any cast members or any sketches from *SNL*. I mean that I couldn't remember any *words*.

I kept smiling, and Lorne Michaels clarified his question. "I don't mean that you grew up working on the show," he said. "Like how someone grows up in the circus."

"Yeah, like I'm the sword swallower!" I shouted.

"But what era of the show did you grow up watching?" he continued.

The only words in the universe that entered my head in that moment were these: "Gilda Radner." Luckily, Gilda Radner was definitely a cast member of *Saturday Night Live*. But unluckily for me, she was a cast member from 1975 to 1980. I was twenty-eight years old at the time of that meeting with Lorne Michaels, and if I had supposedly grown up watching Gilda Radner on the show, then that would have put me somewhere between forty-five and fifty years old.

However, Gilda Radner was the only name that I could think of. I was ready to say it. I was ready to tell Lorne Michaels that I was not, in fact, in my late twenties, but instead was approaching middle age, when Seth Meyers stepped in.

"Was it Mike Myers? Dana Carvey?" he asked, helpfully.

"*Wayne's World*" was all I said.

I could tell Lorne Michaels was impressed.

The meeting continued, though what we talked about, I might never know. All I do know is that Lorne Michaels mentioned seeing me the following week, and I smiled again. "Yes," I probably said. I thanked both of them for taking the time to meet with me, and then I was escorted to the elevators for one final ride. I turned the mention of seeing me next week over and over again in my head. *What did he mean? Do I have an official audition? Do I have to go in for another round of interviews? Or did he just mean we might see each other at the Seventy-Fourth Street bodega if we both happen to run out of milk at the same time?*

Though I couldn't make full sense of these mysterious words, I walked out of 30 Rock calmly. Then, as soon as I hit Sixth Avenue, I began to run. I ran all the way to Central Park and then I slowed down to a speed walk, all the way to Seventy-Second Street. I felt like soaring! I really *had* just had the meeting of a lifetime. I tried calling my best friend Jo, but nobody answered. It was time to celebrate, so I walked into the Utopia Diner and ordered a large Diet Coke. I reminded myself that I had just decided I should be *celebrating*, so I changed my order to a regular Coke. Life was for the living! Jo called me back, and I told her all four details of the meeting that I could remember at that time. She was as ecstatic and giddy as I was. She asked if I was going out celebrating with my friends. I took one look around at my fellow Utopians—average age: sixty-two; average hair color: bald—and smiled. I told Jo that I already *was* out celebrating with my friends. Then I went home and fell asleep without even removing my tinted Chapstick.

The next day, I was informed by my manager that I would go

the following week to audition in person, at 30 Rock, for Lorne Michaels and all the producers from *Saturday Night Live*.

What?!

I had about five days to prepare for the audition. The good news was that I had been doing *Feeling Sad/Mad with Ellie Kemper* at the UCB for a couple of months, so I already had several characters as options. I was told that we would have five minutes to perform however many characters we wanted, but that at least two characters had to be celebrity impressions.

And now I must interrupt my own story to tell you a little bit about Love.

You might remember a certain man of mine, a robust Jewish gentleman of Eastern European descent named Michael Koman. Or, maybe you don't remember him—because Reader, *I have not yet told you all that much about him.* Sure, I have alluded to him here and there—"my boyfriend," "my fiancé," "Michael"—but what more could you be expected to know? Reader, you should know that *he is a comedy writer*. This information will come in handy in about two paragraphs. But you should also know this: like many couples, Michael Koman and I dated for several years before we got married. And yet, at the time of this whirlwind week of mine, Michael and I happened to have been on what is commonly known as "a break." We thought that we might be better off as friends.

We couldn't have been more wrong!

Nonetheless, at the time, we thought that we were right, and we continued to talk on the phone as friends almost daily. And so, when I arrived at 30 Rock the afternoon of my meeting with Lorne Michaels, I called someone who also had "Michael" in his name: Michael. "Michael," I whispered on the phone just before entering the turnstile to get on the elevator. "I am about to meet with Lorne Michaels in his office." I could hear my friend Michael sniffle. He paused. I imagined that his emotions must be engulfing him, and that he was overcome with happiness for me. I opened my mouth to tell him that I was fine, that I would calm down, but he spoke first. "That's amazing, El," he croaked. I smiled, instantly soothed. "I think I'm getting a cold," Michael went on.

Oh, Cupid, you devil you!

Though Michael was battling some mild summer sneezes that particular afternoon, he made a masterful recovery in the days to come. And he spent endless hours speaking to me on the phone about characters, monologues, bits, and other ideas for my audition. We met for coffee, lunch, and one evening of pie. From a comedy standpoint, his help was invaluable, and as a friend, Michael was as supportive as someone possibly could be. At one point over a bad omelette at the Village Den, I realized that I was no longer concerned with the outcome of my *SNL* audition. I just felt very happy that Michael was in my life.

But then I left the diner to get on the subway and realized that if I didn't absolutely nail this audition I would kill myself.

I knew the day that I was auditioning—Thursday, August 7—but I did not find out the exact time until that morning. At 10 a.m., my manager emailed me to say that I should arrive at 30 Rock at four, but that my audition wouldn't be for a while after that. Their hair and makeup department would get us ready, we would fill out paperwork, and then we would wait. I decided to arrive by two, a full two hours early, you know, just to be safe. Before getting on the train, I bought a turkey and cheese sandwich from Fairway. I sat down on a bench outside the grocery store and began to eat. As I was opening my mouth to take a second bite, I noticed that tucked inside the folds of smoked turkey was a dead grasshopper. *A grasshopper.* If you know *anything* about life or omens or insects, you will know that a grasshopper is *the universal symbol of good luck.* I threw my head back and laughed with all the joy there was to have in this world. Then I smashed the grasshopper repeatedly with my foot and threw the sandwich into the street. I mean, I had almost just eaten a grasshopper! Disgusting! I dug through my backpack until I found a squashed S'mores Luna Bar, made sure there weren't any bugs in it, and headed for the train.

As soon as I arrived at 30 Rock, I went to the hair and makeup room on the eighth floor. After that, I was led to a large, windowless room where I filled out what must have been forty-five minutes' worth of paperwork. Then, I sat in a chair next to maybe eighteen other actors. I knew Nate Lang and John Mulaney from UCB, but I didn't recognize anyone else. Maybe they were from LA or Chicago? Had they also referred to Lorne Michaels as Michael Lornes? There was no way to know for sure.

Eventually, someone led us downstairs, one by one, to a dressing room outside the studio. Because commentary on the 2008 Summer Olympics was being broadcast from the *SNL* studios in 8H, we auditioned in *Late Night with Conan O'Brien*'s studio in 6A. 6A! A familiar face, at last! I had only been in that studio a handful of times doing bits on *Conan*, but it was reassuring to be in a space that felt—well, not quite like home, but like a studio I had performed in a few times before.

John Mulaney auditioned just ahead of me. We passed each other in the narrow hallway between the stage and the main floor, and he told me that he felt like all energy had just left his body. He was done. I was next. I would be able to feel like all energy had just left my body in a matter of minutes. I was in the home stretch!

I performed five characters that evening. My two celebrity impressions were Miley Cyrus and Renée Zellweger, and my three showcase characters were Miss Sullivan, a terrified substitute teacher; Taya, an eccentric frozen yogurt server; and Mary, a woman on a trip in Tahiti breaking up with her husband back home in Pennsylvania. I had come up with the characters of both Taya and Mary that week.

And suddenly, just like that—my audition was over. All I remember is that the lights in the audience were not dimmed, I could see Lorne Michaels and the five or six other people sitting there, and there was pleasant laughter throughout my audition. In fact, though everyone warns you beforehand that no one will laugh during your audition, I have never spoken to any person who has auditioned for *SNL* who has experienced this. That's right. Even the brass enjoys a chuckle, guys!

I left the building feeling drained. I was so tired. All energy and any reserves had indeed been completely zapped from my system. But do you know what often saves you when energy cannot?

A crazy little thing called Love.

That same night, a bunch of Conan writers were meeting up at Hurley's, a three-floor saloon. Michael had texted me to see how the audition went and invited me to join them. Reader, *I married him*. Four years later. That night, *I met him at Hurley's*. The Conan gang and Michael and I shared some brews and classic pub grub, and when I finally fell asleep that night, I felt very happy. Not only because if I ever met with Lorne Michaels again I would know exactly what era of *SNL* I had grown up on (*Wayne's*

World), but also because somebody else must have paid for our appetizers—I never got a bill and no bartender stopped me on the way out! Mostly, though, I was happy because I had spent the evening laughing with Michael.

But I never did hear back from *Saturday Night Live*, so I'm guessing I didn't get the part.

Hulk

One Sunday morning in the spring of 2010, my then-boyfriend, now-husband Michael and I went to a very healthy, very hip restaurant in NoHo. NoHo, for those readers not from New York City, is the area *north* of *Houston* Street—see what they did there? Technically, it should be called NoHoSt, I guess, but nobody would really know how to pronounce that, and besides, then we wouldn't be able to say "ho" and get away with it!

Besides saying "ho" and giggling afterward, I also used to really love brunch. I now understand that brunch is either just breakfast, or it is just lunch, depending on what you order. Nobody came up with any new items for this concept; everyone just puts everything on the menu at once, and we all call ahead to try to get a table before being told that they do not take reservations. Anyway, to every meal there is a season, and in the spring of 2010, I still slept past 6:00 a.m. on weekends, I did not realize that lemon ricotta pancakes cost twice as much but taste just the same as regular pancakes when smothered in syrup, and neither Michael nor I was quite out of our "Can you believe we actually live in the same city as the girls from *Sex and the City*? I'm a Miranda!" phase.[1] For these reasons, we spent that Sunday morning eating brunch.

1 Michael was (is) a Miranda. I was (am) a Carrie.

While not a certifiable health *nut*, I do genuinely like wholesome meals, preferring to save my indulgences for normal late-night desserts—traditional treats like an entire bear and a half of Stauffer's Animal Crackers eaten alone on the floor with the lights off and the shades drawn. So, for this brunch, I selected the entrée titled Quinoa & Lentils. While the fine print below read "delicata squash, sautéed greens, housemade burrata, and poached egg," I figured the two primary ingredients of "Quinoa & Lentils" would be quinoa and lentils. I like both of these foods, and—I offer this in my defense—I was looking forward to eating them.

As our waiter walked away and Michael and I tucked into the *New York Times*—for him: the *Book Review*, for me: pretending to read the front page while wishing it was a Word Jumble—a young couple sat next to us. I thought I recognized the woman as the little sister of someone I went to high school with, but I wasn't sure. She never looked my way, and I wondered if I had the disorder where you can't recognize people's faces. Then I went back to wishing I had a Word Jumble.

About ten minutes later, a different waiter brought our food. I knew this not because of what must have been his different face, but because—unlike our first waiter—this man smelled like a vanilla cake. It was heavenly, and exactly how I imagine Gisele Bündchen must smell. As he walked away, I noticed there was something missing from my Quinoa & Lentils: the lentils. I rubbed my eyes and squinted like I was a cartoon character. No lentils. I saw greens, I saw burrata, I saw poached egg. I even saw what I could only presume was the squash—being very fine and very fragile in appearance—and it suddenly became clear to me that *delicata* must mean "delicate" in a foreign language. But I realized I no longer cared about words. Where were the lentils?

"What in the *world*?!" I hissed, slamming my fist on the table and grabbing Michael by the collar. "Look at this food," I snarled, yanking his face toward my plate. My future husband struggled to break free, but my hold was too strong. "I ordered a dish with lentils, Michael, but *do you see any lentils*?" Michael pleaded with me, "Let me go, Ellie. I didn't make the food. I'm sure it was a misunderstanding. I know that we can straighten this out. Just—please let me go." I bared my teeth at him and growled. "Fine," I said. "Fine, Michael." I shoved his face away and punched the air. "But some wise guy is going to pay for this!!!"

The truth is, I tend to get flustered when I'm hungry, or when a meal isn't what I thought it was going to be. One time, when I was seventeen, my sister, Carrie, and I took our nine-year-old brother, Billy, to dinner at TGI Fridays in the St. Louis Galleria. I think that my parents had gone out for the evening, so we assumed this would be a fun thing to do. "Assumed" is right! The "ass" was made not only of "u" and "me," but of Carrie and Billy, too. Our food didn't arrive for more than *an hour* after we ordered. Twenty minutes in, I put my head down on the table and told Carrie to wake me up when the meal came. I knew that if I didn't calm my mind in that moment, I might grow violent. When Billy started in on some story about soccer practice, I grabbed his hand. "Billy, my boy," I said, trying very, very hard to be gentle with my little baby brother. "I need you not to talk." I took Carrie's hand, too. "I need there to be complete silence while my head is down." Billy looked at Carrie, who nodded. Carrie is the very portrait of patience, with an incredibly high threshold for pain. Once, during a game of hide-and-seek when Carrie was four or five, she hid under a pop-up trundle bed in my room. Our neighbor Emily, the seeker, came along and sat on the bed, not knowing Carrie was underneath. But the bed was in the unlocked position, and it collapsed on top of Carrie. Determined to keep her hiding spot, Carrie lay quietly under the fallen bed, stoically enduring not only its weight, but the weight of Emily's gangly body as well. Twenty minutes later, Emily finally caught sight of a small pink shoelace peeking out beneath the metal frame and yelped. "I found you, Carrie!!!" she shouted. Carrie stuck out her small hand and congratulated Emily on her win.

Unfortunately, I share neither my sister's forbearance nor my younger brother's childlike wonder. In addition to getting angry when I am hungry, I also do not find it easy to adapt to changes in plans. And I had been counting on those lentils. I'm not sure I was wrong in doing that—the dish was named *Quinoa & Lentils*. Suddenly, the universe was spinning. For someone like me, changes like this are upsetting. I become unmoored. Like a bird sitting in a tree and the tree is suddenly cut down, or a bird flying through the air and the air is suddenly filled with kites, I feel out of control, I panic, and I accidentally fly straight into a closed window.

Plans, schedules, and structure make me feel secure in a world that—let's just say it—is going straight to hell. I have loved schedules for as long as I can remember. To prove to you that this is true, here is a schedule I made when I was seven:

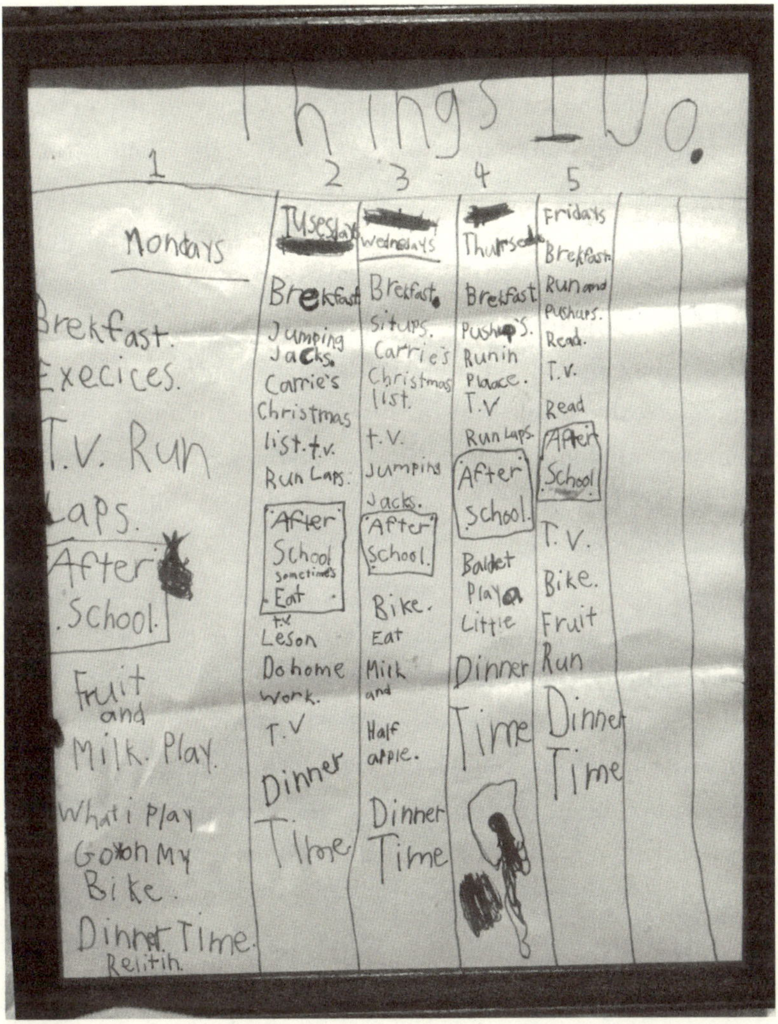

You can see that not only was the concept of weekends nonexistent in my childhood view of the world, but that I accomplished more before Conway School's start time than most adults do in a day. The point is, I like order and plans, I was obsessed with making Carrie's Christmas List (as her literate older sister, I was this toddler's eyes and ears), and "Relith" was code for "Religion" (my parish School of Religion class on Monday evenings).

Back at brunch, I took a deep breath. I knew that you catch more flies with honey, and so I was ready to be a one-woman army of bees.

I caught the eye of our original waiter, the one who didn't smell like vanilla cake, and waved. He walked over to our table, and I laid my hand gently on his arm. "Is everything okay?" he asked. I guess he wasn't used to customers touching him—and I quickly realized that was because it was totally inappropriate. I removed my hand. "Everything's okay," I said softly, showing him the bowl. "I think there are supposed to be lentils with this quinoa, but there's only quinoa."

Well trained, the waiter expressed concern and announced that he would go get his manager. This was not part of the plan; I noticed people beginning to look over. My initial outburst with Michael could have been described as "stormy," but it had also been reasonably quiet. Now, the waiter's loud voice was getting the attention of my fellow patrons, and I imagined what they must be thinking. "*Mom, today I saw a grown woman cry because she didn't get what she ordered at brunch*," one of them would recount on an afternoon phone call home. "*You've got to move out of New York City*," this wise mom would reply.

The only thing more embarrassing than losing your temper is losing your temper *for all the world to see.* Our waiter's pledge to get the manager combined with my rapidly dropping blood sugar was laying all the necessary groundwork for what you might call *a scene.* As though I were listening to a C+C Music Factory album from 1990, beads of perspiration started dripping from my armpits, trickling down my back, and soaking through my high-rise Hanes. I clung to the notion that I could still make honey—remember how earlier I called myself a one-woman army of bees?—and be nice. But the intestinal gas now forming as a result of having coffee on an empty stomach suggested otherwise. I was beginning to lose control. My legs trembled and I felt light-headed. I looked at Michael, helpless. "What is happening to me?" I whispered, my mouth dry and my eyes large. "Michael? Things are about to get ugly." My future husband held my gaze. "Baby, I am here for you," he declared. "But I do want to wash my hands before I eat." Michael then left for the bathroom. I tried some light breathing exercises, but I knew I had no idea what I was doing. I have read in many places that breathing can calm a person down, but I have also read that running will both extend your life and kill you prematurely. The point is, you can't believe everything you read. I think that's why I like Word Jumbles so much.

With Michael gone, I had no one to turn to besides the waiter who smelled like cake. I waved him over and asked him to please go stop the first waiter from getting the manager. "Who is this other waiter?" he asked, hurt. But I couldn't answer. I could feel my muscles expanding.[2] A button popped off my jeans.[3] I was turning green.[4] I opened my mouth to speak, but a roar came out instead.[5]

I had reached Hulk status.

A middle-aged woman approached the table. She did not smile. "I'm the manager. Is there a problem?" Her jaw was clenched, and her eyes narrowed. The young lady at the table next to us, the one who I thought was the little sister of the girl

2 Because the intestinal gas was stretching out my stomach.

3 Because my gassy stomach was so bloated.

4 Because I felt sick.

5 Actually, it was just a grossly loud burp.

I went to high school with, was now staring directly at me, and suddenly my inability to recognize faces was cured, and I saw with absolute certainty that Deirdre Walsh, captain of the 2001 John Burroughs Varsity Swim Team, would be a full witness to the fury flag I was about to let fly. "Hi, Deirdre!" I shouted. "Do you live in New York now?"

I turned back to the manager. I briefly closed my eyes and tried to envision a placid lake, or a sunset in Tahiti. But all I could envision were lentils, quinoa, and birds falling out of the sky!

"Yes, there is a problem," I said tightly. "There aren't any lentils in this Quinoa and Lentil dish."

The manager looked down at my bowl. She picked up a fork and moved some things around. "See this?" she asked me, pointing to a teensy-weensy flake of food. "That's a lentil." She stared at me for a moment. "Lentils are disc-shaped legumes that come in all sorts of sizes and colors."

And now we have reached the last of my three most adorable quirks. As we have already established, I get irritated when I'm hungry. I don't easily adapt to changes in plans. And, finally, *I don't like being sassed*. I guess I don't know anyone who actually *enjoys* being sassed, as that is the whole point of sassing—the sasser seeks to weaken the sassee with his sass. But some people laugh off this pain. You've heard of the song "The Tears of a Clown"? This is all about the pain that people try to laugh off. But I don't try to laugh off pain. I try to get even!!!

"Oh, I know what lentils look like," I said icily. I was smiling, but it was the smile of a madwoman. "I know that they are discs. What are you pointing to in here?" She looked at me again and asked if she could use my spoon. I told her that she could. She then *lifted out a tiny shell of a lentil, a sliver so small you would be better off feeding it to a planarian.* "This is a lentil," she told me.

I then saw that the dish was sprinkled with these little slivers, probably two dozen or so in total. *So, these are the lentils*, my brain told me. *This is what all the fuss has been about*. At the end of the day: the lentils had been there all along. They just weren't what I was expecting. And suddenly I was exhausted. I looked wearily at Deirdre Walsh and sighed.

A lentil is never just a lentil, is it? But in this case, it really was (or wasn't). I thanked the manager for her help and told her that the dish wasn't quite what I had been expecting, but that it looked delicious all the same. Was some of me behaving well because I could see that the sunny blond John Burroughs swimmer was watching, and I didn't want her to tell everyone from home that I was psychotic? Yes. Was another part of me behaving well because, deep down, I knew that none of this really mattered? Also yes. But was the greatest part of me behaving well so that everyone would just go away, and I could finally put food in my face? Absolutely.

Bride

I couldn't have known, that morning on the elevator in 2005, that the stubbly man next to me wondering aloud if almond croissants contain enough protein to make any difference would end up as my husband. There was no way I could have guessed that the spectacled houseguest asking my mom if she was absolutely positive she had roasted the Thanksgiving turkey at a high enough temperature would become my life partner. How could I have predicted that the weepy guy beside me during *The Dark Knight* ("The Joker's henchman just threw the bomb off the boat in order to save people's lives," he sobbed. "He defied the Joker in the name of peace!") would eventually be the father of my son? And yet, as we have recently established, Love works in mysterious ways. Love was definitely on our side on July 7, 2012, which is the day that Michael Koman and I got married, and also the day that I accidentally told Leo Rusnack that I loved him. I had not met Leo Rusnack until that night—he was an eighty-four-year-old guest from the groom's side—but I was caught up in the spirit of things, I was overly excited, and Leo Rusnack happened to be at the right place at the right time.

I am not sure that my husband's twelve-year-old self could have imagined this would be where he ended up. At that time, Michael was probably trying out his stand-up jokes on an audience of Mariana fruit bats. His parents had gotten divorced when he was eight, and his father had moved across the world to the island of Saipan, a US commonwealth in the Western Pacific, several years later. Michael spent four summers there, from ages twelve to sixteen, and still speaks fondly of it.

When I was twelve, I had just starred as Cathy, a poor man's Rizzo, in our sixth-grade production of *Happy Valley High*, a poor man's *Grease*. I had a crush on an inscrutable redhead named Adam Smith, I had just started using Clean and Clear Spot Treatment to stave off acne, and I couldn't wait for ninth grade, so I could be a cheerleader.

Michael started doing stand-up at The Comedy Store in La Jolla, California, while he was still a sophomore in high school. He was working at the club's front desk as a ticket taker when Fred Burns, the club's manager, asked him if he wanted to give stand-up a whirl. Michael said yes, and his first act was done entirely in a fake British accent. Art is complicated, and it is impossible to say where or how Michael came up with this character; he modestly claims it happened "on a whim." Afterward, Michael returned home to binge-eat Snickers bars and binge-watch comedy movies—*Twentieth Century*, *Road to Utopia*, *Sherlock, Jr.*—until after midnight.

In tenth grade, I played field hockey in the fall and ran track in the spring. I went to the Blue and Gold homecoming dance with Justin Kram, I got my driver's license in May, and I said "No!" when offered pot at a U2 concert that summer. I was also really good at Algebra II.

Michael and I are very different. I, for example, place great emphasis on manners, appearing engaged in social situations, and never letting there be lulls in conversations. Michael, in contrast, is extremely comfortable with blank facial expressions, speaking quietly and unintelligibly, and lots of silence. My family belonged to a country club and took long summer road trips to visit my grandma and grandpa in Ridgewood, New Jersey. Michael went on cruises on the Black Sea with his mother and stepfather and was once babysat in La Jolla by a Mormon couple who built a "healing pyramid" over his bed with a crystal dangling from the apex.

How will these two lovebirds meet? you wonder.

We met when Michael was a twenty-eight-year-old writer at *Late Night with Conan O'Brien* and I was a twenty-five-year-old intern. Thankfully, gainful employment was not something Michael seemed particularly concerned with in a companion. We became close pals, hanging out on weekends and going to improv shows and dinner. I told my mom that I wasn't sure if he had a crush on me or not; there certainly weren't any other guys in my life with whom I hung out so exclusively and so often. I sort of had a crush on Michael, but mostly I was glad to have such a good friend.

Michael met my family in St. Louis before we were even dating. It was a cold and dreary autumn, and the great Writers' Strike of 2007–2008 was in full swing. Across the nation, writers from television and movies were seriously considering going out in the light winds and intermittent drizzle to picket, before deciding that eating lunch at a diner made more sense. *Late Night* always had shows over the Thanksgiving holiday; Michael was supposed to have been stuck in NYC working that week and unable to go home to San Diego, so his mother and stepfather had planned a trip to Europe. By the time the strike was announced, it was too late for them to cancel their trip, so I invited Michael to spend the holiday with my own family. This was odd because Michael was not my boyfriend, nor was it characteristic of me to invite people to do things. I hadn't expected him to say yes when I invited him, but he did. The next thing I knew, he was sidling up to my dad, a banker and former high school football quarterback, asking him quietly if the tap water in St. Louis is safe to drink.

I had introduced Michael as my friend, which he was, but I think my whole family was confused. "Ellie," my mom said, as she mashed the potatoes and I watched. "Are you two dating now?" I considered the question. "No," I replied. "Think of him as Jo," I explained, referring to my best friend from college. Of course, Michael wasn't Jo; he was a man no one in my house had ever met who was now sleeping on an air mattress in Billy's room. Nonetheless, the visit went off without a hitch—though I think we all left that weekend wondering what, exactly, had just happened.

It was on the eve of my breakthrough role as Sue, the negligent veterinarian's assistant in a training video for veterinarian assistants, that Michael and I decided we should start dating for real. Was Michael swept away by my performance as the crabby employee who didn't care about pets? Could've been. Whatever the reason, we clicked, and three years later, in August 2011, Michael proposed to me; we set our wedding date for the following July.

I had never been a bride before, but I haven't been a lot of things before; inexperience doesn't exactly intimidate me. While I hadn't grown up fantasizing about my wedding day, I also hadn't grown up thinking that I would marry anyone other than Ted Danson. My point is, fantasies and thoughts change over time, and also, I used to have an enormous crush on Ted Danson—despite never having watched an entire episode of *Cheers*.

I accepted my new role of Bride with the dignity and grace it deserved. I knew that this undertaking would require a good deal of endurance, and I "vowed" (wedding pun) to take the planning process in stride. As you might have surmised by now, Reader, I have a tendency to become, ah, *charmingly consumed by* even the simplest of tasks, and I didn't want my wedding to become a mess of anxious meltdowns. *Slow and steady wins the race*, I thought to myself during a stress-reducing hike in LA's Griffith Park. *Be the tortoise bride—not the hare.* And yet even a sunny hike in a vast park where severed heads are occasionally found was not enough to bring me inner stillness. The truth is, I felt completely overwhelmed by the idea of planning a wedding. I knew that I wanted a traditional affair with a Catholic ceremony—but I also knew that the biggest party I had planned up until that point was the night I invited four friends over to watch the 2006 Oscars. A wedding would be a party on a different scale; there was no getting around it. Even if I were to keep the guest list to a minimum of family only, that would still be more than five dozen guests—all of them looking vaguely like Michael or me. The seemingly endless decisions before me—meal selections, floral arrangements, venues, invitations—struck fear deep into my heart, and I began to panic.

I realized that if I did not attempt to exist on a plane of utter and complete serenity, I would never be able to get through the process of planning my wedding without going crazy. And so I decided to enroll in a class on Transcendental Meditation (TM). I had first heard about TM from Michael himself. He had lived in Los Angeles in his early twenties, spending a great deal of time driving around in an old Jeep Wrangler, listening to Leonard Cohen, and meditating; in my early twenties, I had spent a great deal of time driving around in a champagne-colored Taurus, listening to Matchbox 20, and playing recreational field hockey. But even the powerful '90s hits "3AM" and "Push" failed to give me the kind of mystical stillness I was now seeking, so I decided to give TM a try.

The basement of the Los Feliz TM Center I chose was warm, and there were always clementines around. *At the very least*, I thought, smiling to myself, *you won't get scurvy.* I had learned when I was just a girl that pirates at sea often suffered from scurvy due to a lack of vitamin C. And while I was more than ready to embrace the spirit of a pirate as I planned my wedding (*"Let's bustle this dress, mateys! Arrr!"*), I was not ready to get sick from being deprived of fresh fruit. Put an eye patch on me and hand over the cutlass, sure, but don't you dare take away my vitamins!

However, my TM class ended up being about much more than citrus; it ended up being about naps. While the class stretched a full three days, I had learned all that I was to learn within the first ten minutes. The main lesson was my mantra, which I am not allowed to reveal here because the ruler of Transcendental Meditation forbids followers from ever sharing their mantras. As a hint, though, mine rhymes with "phlegm." For the purposes of this story, let's just say that my mantra *is* "phlegm."

Here is what those crucial first ten minutes taught me to do. I would inhale deeply and say "phlegm" in my head. Then, I would exhale (but I wouldn't say "phlegm"). I would do all of this while sitting quietly with my eyes closed. If another thought entered my head while I was breathing and saying "phlegm," I would acknowledge the thought but not pay it any mind. "Picture that thought like a little puppy dog nipping at you," my TM instructor advised us. "Smile at the dog, but continue your walk." Even though I had never owned a pet—which is, incidentally, precisely why I was able to endow Sue from the veterinarian video with just the right amount of indifference—I was able to understand what my teacher was getting at. *Ignore the thought*, I thought to myself any time I started to get distracted by a random thought. *Phlegm*, I would think instead and breathe in. Then I would say nothing silently but still breathe out. And then I would do it again for what felt like twenty minutes (our instructor cautioned us against using an actual timer), after which I was supposed to slowly open my eyes and readjust to the real world.

There was just one problem with closing my eyes and reciting this mantra—I soon began falling asleep within two or three minutes of closing my eyes. I'm not sure that's a huge surprise; I was in a warm room that smelled like oranges. Who wouldn't fall asleep under those circumstances? When I practiced at home, it was even worse. At first, I meditated on my bed, but quickly learned that was just asking for a nap. I tried sitting on the hardwood floor, but it turns out I could nap on that, too. I tried the front seat of my car, the backseat of my car, an uncomfortable garden stool, and even standing up. But I was able to fall asleep in all of these locations.

Have I officially reached nirvana? I had to wonder.

Whenever a wedding task would come my way, I could feel my heart rate begin to rise. *Slow down*, I urged myself. *Remember the mantra*. And I would close my eyes, quietly say "phlegm," then wake up anywhere between fifteen minutes to four hours later.

"El, have you put together your guest list?" my mom wrote one December afternoon. "I'm attaching the names and addresses of friends Dad and I would like to invite." I smiled as I read my mom's email. I knew that the guests would come, whether notified or not. Guests have a way of figuring that sort of thing out. "Don't worry, Mom," I wrote back. "The guests will come." "I'm not worried," she responded. "I just want to make sure you invite my friends." I closed my eyes for a moment and said "phlegm." "We've got this," I wrote to my mom. "What?" she said.

"Ellie, do you need help finding your dress?" my sister asked me a few days later. I giggled. I had asked Carrie to be my maid of honor, but I feared she was getting too caught up in the minutiae. "I'll be wearing a dress that day," I answered mysteriously. "Right," she replied. "Do you want me to go shopping with you? That could be fun!" I laughed again and took her hand in mine. "Stop worrying," I whispered, mostly to myself.

"Ellie, are we signed up for Pre-Cana?" Michael asked me one weekend at brunch. "Don't Catholics have to do Pre-Cana in order to be married in the church?" I took another bite of eggs and ruffled Michael's hair. "We'll get married in the church," I assured my Jewish fiancé. "All of the religious stuff will sort itself out," I added, waving to the waiter for more pineapple juice.

Every piece of my wedding did sort itself out, in fact, and that is because my mom and my sister sorted every single piece of it out for me. *They're doing a great job*, I thought to myself during a meeting about flowers. I pretended to listen to the florist for another few minutes, nodding at Carrie and pointing to a hydrangea.

Through my disciplined practice of TM, I had reached a previously unknown plane of transcendental napping. I was able to fall asleep at a moment's notice, regardless of my surroundings, and irrespective of my companions. I woke up calm, relaxed, and ready for another nap. *Nirvana is your closest family and friends doing all of your work for you*, I realized, no longer possessing the energy to do any of the wedding work myself. "Ellie, you're drooling again," my instructor said with a sigh. I shook myself awake. "Sorry," I murmured. "I go deep," I explained, gathering my bags and leaving the complimentary refresher course that was included with the TM package I had originally purchased.

When my wedding day finally arrived, and all the suspense was finally over, I gave Michael a hug. "We did it," I told him. I saw my mom and Carrie out of the corner of my eye and gave them a "hang ten" sign. "Couldn't have done it without you, babes!" They frowned. "Everyone is out there waiting for you to cut the cake," my sister said, sighing. "Why are you in the kitchen?" she added wearily.

Later that night, Michael's mom would see Paul McCartney as she walked back to her hotel in the rain. I would eat an entire large pizza, alone and in silence, watching the sun come up as Michael slept in his tuxedo. Leo Rusnack would wonder if I had been, in fact, the one that got away, and our photographer would privately remark to himself that he had never seen so much sweat on a bride's neck.

As for my dance with Transcendental Meditation, it was slowing from a cha-cha to a waltz. The next week, the lights would go out in the ballroom completely. I found that I no longer needed to turn to TM to calm my mind; as a now-wife, I found that tranquility by telling my husband everything that he does wrong instead. Look, I don't know why relationships work. I just know that ours does.

Receptionist

My voice has not been described as "warm" or "professional-sounding" as often as it has been described as "please speak more quietly," so it is a testament to my skill as an actor that I successfully played a receptionist in an office for more than four years on NBC. "How did you do it, Ellie?" a lot of people have not asked me. "Were the computers on set actually connected to the internet?" more people want to know.

Yes, the computers on the set of *The Office* were most definitely connected to the internet, and here are some of the items that I purchased while sitting in the background:

- A sky-blue chevron rug from Gilt.com
- A Stanley 65-Piece Homeowner's Tool Set (funny because there is a character on the show named Stanley—but the tool set had nothing to do with him)
- Tickets to numerous shows at the Upright Citizens Brigade on Franklin Avenue
- My dinner order from Pimai It's Thai! to pick up on my way home from work
- My dress for the 2011 Emmys
- An antique horn-grip corkscrew for my father-in-law
- A framed map of San Francisco as a Christmas present for

my little brother, Billy. Rainn Wilson could not *believe* that I bought such a "lame" (his word) gift for a twenty-three-year-old man. "Why don't you get him something that he would like?" he demanded. I told Rainn that not only did Billy live in San Francisco, but that I was also giving him the gift of latitude and longitude. "It's never a bad idea to know where you are," I pointed out. Rainn responded by showing me eight new tech items that were popular at the time—Apple iPad Mini, Apple iPhone 5, Apple MacBook Pro, and five others that I would never be able to remember—and suggested that I purchase one of those for Billy instead. "You're an actress on a TV show," he told me. "Billy thinks you're a billionaire." I laughed and gave Rainn a pat on the shoulder. The poor guy just couldn't understand that love and maps from the One Kings Lane clearance section were greater than money.

Here is the map in Billy's childhood bedroom, still unopened as of Christmas 2017:

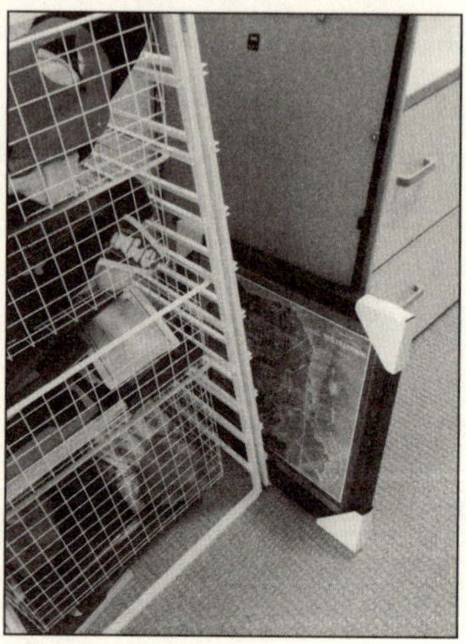

A lot of other people ask me, "Did it feel like *The Office* was a master class in comedy?" To these people I say, "Hey, man! I don't go to *your* office and ask *you* if *your* job is a master class!" But once those people are gone, I take off my thug façade and breathe a giant sigh of relief. To be totally honest, I knew what they were getting at; I was just acting tough in case they tried to rob me. How could a show like that *not* be a master class in comedy? And why is everyone in this paragraph so obsessed with using the term "master class"? In terms of comedy giants, I realize that the Dunder Mifflin fans out there will point to the usual suspects—Steve Carell, Mindy Kaling, Ed Helms, Jenna Fischer—but I would like to offer up two names with which you might not be as familiar: Lee Eisenberg and Gene Stupnitsky. These writer-producers from the show appeared in an episode called "Café Disco," playing two Vance Refrigeration employees who spy Kelly and Erin dancing together. The dialogue goes:

Leo (played by Gene): There's girls in there.
Gino (played by Lee): Where?
Leo: The other room.
Gino: What other room?
Leo: Down the hall.
Gino: There's girls in there?
Leo: What'd I just say?
Gino: You get me my sandwich?
Leo: Forget the sandwich. Girls! *Girls!*

And I have never seen two men more naturally funny than they are in that exchange. Anyway, Jim Carrey and Will Ferrell also made cameos on *The Office*, so yes, if it will stop your incessant questioning, you can call it a master class in comedy.

The remaining people, the ones who have asked about neither the internet connection nor the master class, are several extended-family members who feel the need to remind me periodically that they never watched *The Office* because it made them both cringe and feel carsick at the same time. I look at these extended-family members, and I nod, and I tell them, "Yes, you have mentioned that before." And as I stick out my tongue at those family members once their backs are turned, I recall some of the great observations I made during my time on that show. Were these revelatory life lessons? Sensible instructions for navigating a ruthless world? Eternal wisdom that I would, in time, pass on to my descendants? They were not. Instead, they were the following truths that have no real practical application to daily life:

1) Only Steve Carell can touch the bagels.

On my first day of work on *The Office*, I did not use serving tongs to select my bagel from the platter at craft service. I noticed that there *weren't* any serving tongs or spoons at craft service, so I selected the bagel with my eyes, and then I leaned forward to grab it with my hand. I was careful to touch *only* the bagel that I wanted, because I understood that touching the other bagels would be unsanitary. But at the same time that my hand had reached the sesame bagel of choice, another hand, a much larger hand, seized my own. I looked up, terrified! A powerfully built Armenian man was staring back at me. "You do not get to use your hands!" he cried. "Only Steve Carell gets to use his hands!" I swallowed hard. I wasn't sure who this man was, but his grip was fierce, and his face was perspiring.

"I'm so sorry," I squeaked. "I didn't see any tongs." The large hand pointed, and the strong man frowned. "The tongs are at the end of the table!" he shouted. I followed his gaze and there, sure enough, were four black silicone serving tongs. This mighty gentleman with the bearlike paws had been right all along. I walked to the end of the table to get the tongs, but I wasn't sure what to do with them, since I already had the sesame bagel in my hands. So, I selected another bagel, this time a blueberry one, and put both bagels in a paper bowl (because I did not see a plate). "Thank you so much," I said softly.

I never once saw Steve Carell eat a bagel—I only ever saw him quietly take his place at the end of the lunch line most afternoons—but the bagel man's point was that if Steve Carell ever *did* choose to eat a bagel, he would enjoy the unique privilege of *not needing to bother with the tongs.* In the world of show business, even hygiene is a status game, and only when you ascend to the level of national treasure do you earn the distinction of being allowed to touch food with your bare hands. (P.S.: The so-called bagel man was Vartan Chakirian, the head of craft service. After such an intense first encounter, the two of us would go on to become good friends.)

2) Bryan Cranston is not the same person as Walter White.

I went to see my first musical, *Oklahoma!*, live onstage at the St. Louis Fox Theatre when I was eight years old. I couldn't believe that the dark, brooding villain of the show, a loner named Jud Fry, received a standing ovation when he came out for his bow. "But he was the bad guy!" I protested to my mom. I refused to stand up, and I even stopped clapping my own hands. My mom laughed. "We are applauding the actor, not the character," she told me. "The actor did a tremendous job!" I agreed with myself to disagree with my mom and continued to sit in my seat until I saw that I had dropped two peanut M&Ms on the floor. Then I was finally forced to get out of my seat to bend down and reach for the candy so that I could bring it to my face and eat it. But clap for that evil man was something I would never do.

History repeated itself when brilliant chameleon actor Bryan Cranston came to direct the fourth episode of the ninth season of *The Office*. I had not started watching *Breaking Bad* until the show was in its third season, but I had spent the late summer of 2012 largely in its grasp. "This show is as addictive as the meth it is about," I whispered to my husband. I wasn't intentionally trying to be as insightful as a paid television critic, but I can't always stop these gems from slipping out of my mouth; we can all agree that the show is incredible, and Walter White is an antihero for the ages. So, when I saw Bryan Cranston walk onto the Dunder Mifflin parking lot set in early fall, I nearly fainted. I knew that Walter White was a complicated man—neither all bad nor all good—but still, this drug baron was about to take my character and tell her where to stand and when to answer the phone and I was terrified. He greeted our cast and crew with a friendly "Morning, guys!" but I knew not to fall into his trap. *Your smile can't fool me*, I remember thinking. I was so scared he was going to offer me crystal meth. "Just keep me away from the Blue Sky," I muttered to myself. "You keep that Blue Magic away from me," I added, using an alternate name for Walter White and Jesse Pinkman's signature blue and notoriously potent pure crystal methamphetamine. "Baby don't want no Blue!" I shouted at my own reflection in a nearby prop car.

"Who are you talking to?" Brian Baumgartner, who played Kevin, asked.

The title of Bryan Cranston's episode was "Work Bus," but all the cast had secretly nicknamed it "Death Bus." The reason we had given the episode this nickname is that we all nearly died on the bus. I cannot emphasize strongly enough that our collective near-death experience had *nothing* to do with Bryan Cranston. It didn't even have anything to do with drug trafficking. It had to do with the brakes temporarily not working and the bus flying off the side of the road. I remember falling out of my seat and feeling grateful that I no longer had to come up with an excuse for having wet my pants several minutes earlier. (There is a part in "Work Bus" where Jim is leading a song called "Shabooya Roll Call," and I had gotten a case of the giggles during this song, a case so severe that I eventually peed through my panty hose and onto my skirt. Anyway, now I could just blame the urine stains on the impact of the bus crash.) The cast survived the bus flying off the road and, if anything, was made stronger because of it, but I also felt unexpectedly proud now that Walter White could see how tough we all were. Up until then, we had shot only interior scenes in the office bullpen. But now, we were out in the wild, wild west, baby. Try and mess with us now, Walter White!!!

(I do want to mention here that kind, delightful Bryan

Cranston is in no way like Walter White, and that I did give him a standing ovation after *All the Way.*)

3) During downtime on a set, only make small talk if absolutely necessary.

Because I had never worked on anything longer than a commercial or a comedy sketch before joining the cast of *The Office*, I was unaware of just how much time on a film set is spent waiting. You are sitting and waiting, or standing and waiting, or eating and waiting. The one constant is that you are waiting. It's unfair that actors get paid to wait, and other people actually have to do work in order to get paid, but here it might be helpful to remember that actors are more valuable than everyone else in the world.

During these wait times, which happen as a result of lighting setups, or script changes, or costume malfunctions, or a baby that has been written into the episode and won't stop crying (which is why I really don't think babies should be on television, guys), people will start to chat with one another. This is natural and to be expected. And one thing I often compliment myself on is my ability to keep a conversation going. But, as is the case with most talents on which I compliment myself (picking out ripe avocados, sight-reading basic piano tunes, canceling and then rescheduling appointments), this one has a drawback (avocado goes bad by end of day, basic piano tunes are boring piano tunes, eventually have to go to appointment anyway): sometimes the conversation doesn't end. This is a problem because I will often wander into strange, undesirable conversational territory and find myself getting entangled in the vines of the trees that grow there. I can't always seem to get myself out of the vines, and then I am horrified to discover that on top of everything else, I am standing on quicksand! So, I'm tangled up, sinking, and still trying as hard as I can to explain, for some reason, why my sister-in-law's brother's favorite book is *Emma*—with no help in sight!

Once, I was standing next to Kate Flannery, who played Meredith, while our camera guys adjusted some lights in the accounting area. I had some old hand warmers in my coat pocket from a few days earlier, when we had been filming outside. (I should also explain that actresses get much colder than all other people when filming outside, and are often offered those air-activated hand and foot warmers by the wardrobe department. This is a relief, because otherwise the actresses would get even colder.) The hand warmers had long ago gone cold and hard,[1] and I mentioned to Kate how I kept reaching into my pockets and thinking they were old Kleenex. "Actually," I said, taking one of the hand warmers out to examine it, "it really looks like an old maxi pad." Kate laughed and, encouraged, I continued. "Or at least a pantyliner!" Then, Steve Carell walked up to us and asked how our days were going. I turned to Steve Carell and welcomed him into our group. Then, because I see silence as an enemy, I started talking again. "Kate and I were just saying how much this old hand warmer looks like a maxi pad," I shared with Steve Carell. He nodded. "Oh," he said. "I guess it does."

The camera guys finished the lighting setup just then, and our assistant director Kelly called everyone to places. I walked away from Steve Carell and Kate and decided I

1 That's what she said, guys!

should probably just throw the old hand warmers away so nobody would ever have to talk about them again.

4) #18 on the call sheet really means #18 on the call sheet.

For those readers out there unfamiliar with the term "call sheet," this is the piece of paper on a television or film production that tells you what scenes are being shot that day and in what order. In addition, it contains all the names and job titles of the cast and crew involved, and usually includes a cute mini-weather report with little sun or thunderstorm icons as well. The actors are numbered, frankly, in order of status: the lead actor is #1, and the rest of the cast falls into line according to either the size of their part, the point in the production timeline at which they joined, or a typo from a production assistant working on the call sheet. When I joined *The Office* at the end of Season Five, I was assigned #18 on the call sheet. "I can vote," I joked to our security guard, Joseph. "Because I'm eighteen," I quickly explained. Joseph got it the first time and smiled. "But you can't drink!" he added, laughing. I then tried to think of another unique feature of being eighteen years old, but I don't think there are any.

In high school, Aiko Eto's mom used to cheer on our field hockey team from the sidelines. "Go, Ellie!" she would shout. "#25 on the field, #1 in our hearts!" She would shout out this catchphrase to all the players, so you had to know that you weren't actually #1 in everyone's hearts—how could all sixteen women simultaneously be #1?—but it made you feel pretty great when you were out on the field.

Because there were more than twenty cast members

on *The Office* and only six people to do all our hair and makeup, I was called in very early to get ready. The actors lower down on the call sheet generally had less work to do during the day, and this schedule allowed the actors higher up on the call sheet to spend less time waiting around to shoot. In those dark hours before dawn, driving north on the 101 in a charcoal Ford Fusion rental, I recalled Mrs. Eto's words. "You might be #18 on the call sheet," I psyched myself up over the smooth chatter of Lakshmi Singh, "but you are #1 in their hearts!"

And yet sometimes even I fell victim to the temptation to whine. One evening on the way home from Van Nuys, I complained to my mom on the phone. "It's really insane," I told her. "This morning I was called in for hair and makeup at five thirty a.m., and I didn't even shoot anything until eleven." My mom was silent. "Anyway, I'm exhausted," I went on. "I've been up a long time." My mom paused one more moment before speaking. "The job you have *is* insane," she agreed. "The job you have is a job most people only dream about having."

I knew then that ~~my mother could never, ever understand how difficult my life was~~ my mom was right.

5) One weird meeting might lead to a failed audition, which then might lead to a better audition.

My first meeting with the producers from *The Office* was in the fall of 2008, a couple of months after I had auditioned for *Saturday Night Live*. Sharon Jackson, my agent extraordinaire, had set a meeting for me with Greg Daniels and Mike Schur, the executive producers and writers of *The Office*. I remember that I wore a blue, short-sleeved dress from Anthropologie that didn't *not* make me look like a French cartoon. I met with Greg first, and then Mike joined about ten minutes later. There were only two chairs in Greg's office, and gallant Mike Schur just sort of crouched on the floor. They told me that they were developing a new show, and at one point, the actor Creed Bratton walked in to get a Coke.

A few weeks after that meeting, I was called back to the offices of *The Office* to read with Allison Jones, the casting director, for a part on this new, untitled show written by Greg and Mike. I did not receive a full script, only the scenes that I would be reading, and I was not sure what the show was about. My character's name was Donna. Greg was also in the room, and after the audition, he told me to feel free to use the audition space to prepare for my one-woman show (which he knew I was performing that night at the UCB).

A few weeks after *that*, my manager called me to tell me that, sadly, I had not gotten the part. "What part?" I asked. "The part that you read for Allison Jones," he told me. "The part of Donna." "But what was that show?" I asked him. "And who is Donna?" "It's a new show," he told me. "Donna is a character in the show." I paused. I took a deep breath. "I thought that was, like, a general audition," I admitted. Now it was my manager who paused. "You know what I mean," I continued. "A sort of overall audition, to show people what I can do, in general." I laughed, but it came out as a sob. "Ellie," my manager said gently, "there is no such thing as a general audition."

The show was *Parks and Recreation*, and a character named Donna would eventually be played by the actress and comedian Retta. I'm still not sure if that is the part that I was auditioning for, or if they just ended up naming a different character Donna, but in any case, I am not Donna. I am, however, using that as the title for my debut indie-rock album (mark my words: "I Am Not Donna" will give clarity to a generation).

A few months after the Donna audition, I got the audition for Kellie on *The Office*. This was originally a four-episode arc and the character would later go by her middle name, Erin, since the office already had a Kelly (Kapoor). But names don't really matter here. What matters here is that I had my audition for *The Office* on the same day that I had two other auditions: one for a pilot by Adam Resnick called *Cop House*, and the other for an American adaptation of a British comedy called *Pulling*. This meant that all my nerves were shared among three different auditions, instead of just one. Also, the logistics of getting from one place to another almost gave me a heart attack. I would go from *The Office* in Van Nuys to *Cop House* in Beverly Hills to *Pulling* in Century City. These three sections of Los Angeles are not close to one another, and I am a terrible driver who has no sense of the dimensions of either her own car or those cars around her. So, channeling my anxious energy into driving, navigating, and not sweating through that same blue Anthropologie French cartoon dress left me uncharacteristically calm for the auditions themselves.

My first audition of the three was for *The Office*, and I read two scenes with Ed Helms. I remembered all my lines perfectly, which usually doesn't happen because I get nervous in auditions. But Ed is one of the most welcoming people on the planet, and though I had never met him before, we had some improv friends in common, and we talked about them for a bit before the audition. This both put me at ease and also reminded me that I am pretty bad at keeping in touch with friends. We went through the scene twice, and my only note was to "ice out Andy" more. See, when the show first introduces Erin, she is pretty chill. She has brown hair, she's good at her job, and she's cool. As the show goes on, Erin evolves into a redheaded rube who has trouble answering the phone correctly. But at the time of the audition, the character was smooth and competent.

My other agent extraordinaire, Priyanka Mattoo, called me a few days after the audition to tell me that I had gotten the part. I could not believe it! The odds of booking a role on any show, anywhere, are so small—and this was a show that I happened to worship. I felt like dancing, but instead I ordered a BLT pizza from Pizzeria Mozza, extra bacon. I did not receive callbacks for *Cop House* or *Pulling*, but I did dent a car in the Wendy O'Brien Casting parking lot while trying to turn into a spot at the wrong angle.

After my arc was supposed to have ended, the writers kept Pam (the previous receptionist) as a salesperson. This meant that Dunder Mifflin *still* needed a replacement receptionist—and in June after we wrapped, I received a contract for seven more seasons on *The Office*. (This was a standard network television contract; there ended up being only four more seasons.) I knew then that I definitely needed to take some sort of driving refresher course. Seven years would mean a lot of dented cars otherwise, and I just wasn't ready for that kind of drama.

6) There ain't no party like a Scranton party 'cause a Scranton party *don't stop.*

After we finished filming the final episode of *The Office* in the spring of 2013, our entire cast and a bunch of the crew were invited to a parade and citywide celebration in Scranton, PA. A lot of the cast had been to Scranton for various events in the past, but this was the first time that we would all be there at the same time.

The citizens of Scranton were some of the warmest, most generous, most enthusiastic Americans I have ever met. Am I running for mayor of Scranton? *Maybe I am.* Then again—no, I am not. I just want to point out how exceptionally nice everyone was. In addition to the parade, they threw us a party at the Backyard Ale House. We had a Q&A panel at PNC Field, and the city organized an unbelievable outdoor concert in downtown Scranton. That Saturday happened to be pristine: breezy, sunny, and not a cloud in the sky. Perhaps most memorably, I asked the lady at Blo in Manhattan to add hair extensions after she blew out my hair on Friday morning, and my hair extensions remained perfectly intact until I returned to the city on Sunday afternoon. If that isn't the sign of a successful weekend, I'm not sure what is.

Guest

In 2009, a dream of mine came true when I joined the cast of NBC's *The Office*. But I had barely settled into the lazy satisfaction of knowing that I was America's favorite sitcom's eighteenth-favorite cast member before realizing that my dream job came with a toll: I would be expected to do publicity, which meant going on talk shows.

Let me explain. Since high school, I have—and I need to say this carefully, because I am now married—deeply *admired* David Letterman. Every weeknight, my sister, Carrie, and I would meet in the kitchen to eat ice cream and let this goofball genius and fellow Midwesterner shape our worldview. This crush wasn't complicated: Dave just made us laugh.

Soon, I developed a habit of judging celebrities based wholly on their interactions with Dave. If he liked them, I became a fan. If he seemed unimpressed, I wrote them off. The worst crime, I learned, was being boring, and I shuddered on behalf of the young, chatterbox starlets whose stories went nowhere.

With dread, I realized the same bar that I had set for celebrities on *The Late Show with David Letterman* would now apply to me. What if *I* turned out to be just another dull, chatterbox starlet on a talk show?

My first major appearance was as the second guest on *The*

Tonight Show with Jay Leno in May 2010. While I was relieved that I didn't have to face the king of my childhood kitchen just yet, I was still a nauseated wreck. In preparation for this essay, I forced myself to find a tape of the episode and watch it. It was like watching my own funeral. Actually, watching my own funeral would have been nicer, because I intend for that occasion to be a spirited celebration of my life—not a series of dry stories told in a poorly chosen dress that revealed more pale thigh than America should ever have to see.

Jay asks me to tell him about myself. I report that I grew up in St. Louis, that I am the only one of my siblings with red hair, and that, speaking of siblings, I have three of them. Pausing, I smile slightly and add, "Or, I *used* to have three siblings." This hangs in the air for a moment, no one being exactly sure what I mean. I do not elaborate; it clearly sounds like something terrible has happened to my family.

In fact, my two brothers and one sister couldn't be more alive. What I meant was that we all "used" to live in St. Louis, and, therefore, I "used" to have three siblings there. But I do not say any of this. Instead, I leave the audience only to guess at the horrors this strange redhead has seen. *And why didn't she choose a longer dress?*

The saving grace of the interview is Garry Shandling. He was the lead guest, and throughout my segment, he chimes in and tries to help. At the time, I worried that he was making fun of me. But it's now clear to me that he's just trying to make the segment entertaining. At one point, seemingly seventy-three hours into my story of giving Jon Hamm a hug at an awards show and getting makeup on his tuxedo, Garry compares that smeared tux to the Shroud of Turin. Neither Jay nor I react. "That was an *excellent* reference," Garry mutters to himself.

It *was* an excellent reference. And it breathed life into an otherwise lackluster piece. As Jakob Dylan, the musical guest, sang about how he had nothing but the whole wide world to gain, I wept softly in the darkness. If only I could have shared the cheery outlook of Bob Dylan's son. Instead, I was a failure. A boring, babbling starlet whom not even consummate talk show host and guest Garry Shandling could rescue.

I received a flood of congratulatory emails after that awkward appearance. Family, friends, and coworkers all maintained that I had been very cheerful. A college friend complimented my posture. This is how people who love you let you know that something has not gone well.

And yet, I now see this failure as a necessity. If I hadn't had the opportunity to sink the SS *Leno* that night, I never would have realized the amount of work that should go into making an entertaining talk show segment. Next time, I vowed to be better prepared.

I made several more talk-show appearances over the coming months, slightly improving each time, and when I was finally invited on *Letterman* in 2012, I was beside myself. I decided that I would feel more confident if I had something to show the audience, rather than relying only on my stories, so I asked the segment producer if we could screen a home movie: a "horror film" titled *The Man Under the Stairs* that I had made two decades earlier with Carrie and, you guessed it, our neighbor Emily Sinclair. The segment producer agreed to put it in the lineup, but she could not guarantee that Dave would bring it up during our interview.

Well, Dave *did* bring it up during our interview, and I nearly lost my mind. There I was, some overexcited fangirl with little business being there at all, sitting next to the man of my talk show dreams. I hardly remember walking out to the desk. I know only that I didn't trip. Looking into Dave's face felt like looking at Abe Lincoln—and believe me, I only mean that in the most exciting way. Dave and Abe are both tall, and they are both legends. And up until that point, they had both been figures I had only read about, seen reenacted, or watched on television. If I had died in the wings after that show, I wouldn't have cared at all. And not only because I would have been dead and therefore unable to care. I would have welcomed death because I would have just spent five minutes and twenty-seven seconds talking to David Letterman, and I wasn't sure how my time on Earth could have gotten much better.

Anyway, nobody died. And from a critic's standpoint, the appearance itself was just fine. Not amazing—but also not a disaster. Which in my book was unthinkably wonderful, because it garnered me the greatest prize I could have hoped for: two invitations to come back. By my third time, in February 2015, Letterman had announced his retirement. For my final appearance on his show, I wanted to do something memorable. (And by that I mean something that mostly only my family, my husband, and I remember.)

This idea rested in the pages of an old Hammacher Schlemmer catalog. I am voluntarily on the mailing list of this company of unexpected gifts, and I wouldn't have it any other way. Paging through it several weeks ahead of my spot, I saw a toaster that imprinted images of people's faces on the bread. I emailed my sister right away, asking if she thought this might be something I could bring on the show. "Order the toaster," she wrote back immediately. "Why the hell not?"

But we weren't exactly sure what the point of the toaster would be. Should I tie it into his retirement? A "toast" to Dave? Now unemployed, he'll have more time for breakfast? Or was this a terrible idea? Was putting David Letterman's face on a piece of toast too creepy?

Seized by a sudden decisiveness, I committed to moving forward with the toaster. Ellyn from Burnt Impressions had toaster elements created with Paul Shaffer's face in one toaster slot, Dave's in the other, in forty-eight hours. The segment producer was on board, but, as with my first appearance, there was no guarantee that Dave would get to the bit.

After a few minutes of my famous B-plus banter with Dave, he said he understood that I had brought a gift. He plopped the toaster on his desk, and I inserted two slices of potato bread. As Paul played some light piano accompaniment, Dave and I watched the toaster for a good two and a half minutes. That was precisely the idea: to waste several minutes of national airtime watching bread toast.

Miraculously, when the toast popped out, you could make out Dave's and Paul's faces. Dave offered some jam and butter, and the three of us ate the most delicious meal of my life.

I know it wasn't Christ's face on a piece of linen cloth, but it *was* Dave's face on potato bread. Thanks to bombing five years earlier, I got to experience a true moment of joy: I did a stupid bit with a comedy hero—and it wasn't boring. Or, it was, but it was boring in a good way.

American

I'm not sure if it was the glimmer of the big-city lights or just the freshness of a new land, but I knew from the moment I stepped off the bus in Hannibal, MO, that I was meant to roam. *Look at the post office*, I thought to myself, my fellow sixth graders clambering and yelling all around me. *And there's the highway, too*. There was a post office and a highway just like in my own hometown of St. Louis, MO, but I may as well have been in a different universe. Everything felt new again in this exotic place, and I was invigorated. "When do we go to the caves?" some adolescent klutz shouted next to me. "Yeah, we wanna see the caves!" echoed his idiot sidekick. I rolled my eyes and smiled at the teachers. *Let's skip the caves and go straight to the Mark Twain Boyhood Home and Museum*, I mouthed to Mrs. Hoffman. *After that, I would really enjoy an opportunity to check out the Mark Twain Memorial Lighthouse and old Nipper Park*, I kept mouthing. "What?" Mrs. Hoffman shouted. "Ellie, are you going to throw up?" A couple of my carsick traveling companions were currently puking at a nearby McDonald's. "No, I just—I'm fine," I replied. "I'm fine, Mrs. Hoffman." I shook my head and chuckled to myself. It's not that I was ashamed of the people I was with; it just felt funny to be the most sophisticated person there.

As an American, I hold many things dear: liberty, free speech, a "seems good enough to me" work ethic. But I also understand that the world is a big place, and big places require exploring. For this reason, I made a promise to myself after that trip to Hannibal to try to see just as much of our world as possible—and I have devised a list of pointers to guide me as I sally forth. Here are a few of them:

Ellie's Rules of Travel

1) Learn the language of the new land.

2) Adopt the customs and dress of the new land.

3) Do not sit still. Get out there! The new land is yours for the taking, and you can't take the new land if you are not walking everywhere and in constant pain. Blisters and blood prove that you actually *did something.*

4) Avoid tourist traps and attractions that might make your trip "easy" or "fun." Nobody ever reached a deeper spiritual level by having a nice time.

The first trip I took outside of the United States was to visit my dad's sister Julie and her husband, Michel, in France. Uncle Michel is a farmer, and the two of them lived with their five young children in a small village in Normandy. I was ecstatic. My grandpa would drive from Kansas City to St. Louis to stay a night at our house, and then he, my brother John, and I would all fly from St. Louis to Paris. My aunt would meet us at Charles de Gaulle Airport, and then we would drive the two hours to Le Mesnil-Mauger in her farm-friendly vehicle.

I was about to enter my freshman year of high school, and I had two years of middle school French under *ma ceinture* ("my belt"). My vocabulary was extensive and my verb tenses pristine. Furthermore, while I understood from *Footloose* that the only true universal language was dance, being able to make myself understood in a foreign language using words in addition to dance moves was a thrilling notion to me. In preparation for my trip, I went over my French textbooks exhaustively. I asked my mom if she wouldn't mind adding some *omelettes* or perhaps a *pain perdu* to the breakfast rotation. I felt sorry for my younger siblings, Carrie and Billy. While John and I would be off devouring La Lucerne Abbey and Mont Saint-Michel, little Carrie and Billy would be stuck drawing imaginary towns on our driveway in pink and green sidewalk chalk. "*Au revoir, ma cherie*,"[1] I whispered to Carrie as John, my grandpa, and I loaded into the minivan. "*Ta coeur est ma coeur*."[2]

I wasn't mad, exactly, to learn that my aunt's household spoke only English at home. My cousins were bilingual, so it made sense that the reason they knew English was from speaking it with their family. Nonetheless, I found the whole thing a tad tacky. "We are in the heart of France," I mumbled to my brother one afternoon as we rode around in my uncle's tractor. "It is really, really bad that we aren't speaking French here." My brother looked at me. "Grandpa doesn't speak much French, so I think it's for his benefit," he said. I held my brother's gaze before turning my attention back to the tractor. "And now, a visit to zee

1 "Good-bye, my dearest."

2 "Your heart is my heart"—this is not an expression used by people who speak French.

cows!" my uncle Michel exclaimed from the driver's seat. "*C'est une bonne idée!*" I cried, desperate for the French to catch on. My brother rolled his eyes, and I began humming "La Marseillaise" loud enough for my uncle to hear.

One afternoon, Aunt Julie asked for my help in the kitchen. Even at my relatively young age, I understood that preparing breakfast, lunch, and dinner for five children, Uncle Michel, Grandpa, John, and me for ten days straight might be annoying. I was more than happy to help my aunt whenever I could—which in this instance was one time, that particular afternoon, for one dinner.

To demonstrate both my respect and my humility, I knew that I needed to dress like an American chef in France might dress: one of those horizontal-striped shirts that mimes wear, and blue jeans. I hadn't brought a horizontal-striped shirt on my trip, because I did not own one, so I asked my younger cousin Emilie if I could borrow one of hers. "Why do you need zis shirt?" she asked me. "I will be preparing the evening meal with your *maman*," I announced. "Somebody needs to feed the family," I added. Emilie didn't have a horizontal-striped shirt, but she did have a carrot-printed tank top that said "Les Carottes!" so I squeezed into it and headed to the kitchen. The tank top was tight—Emilie was eight years old; I was fourteen—but a shirt vaguely about cooking would give me the confidence I needed.

When I appeared in the kitchen, my aunt laughed. "Did your laundry get mixed up with Laurent's?" she asked, referring to her infant son. All good travelers can take a joke, and so I chuckled along with her. "Now, what are we thinking for dinner, Aunt Julie?" I moved on. "A *bouillabaisse*? A *coq au vin*?"

I waited for Aunt Julie to be impressed by my familiarity with French dishes, but let's just say *I'm still waiting*. "I'm making meatloaf," Aunt Julie announced. "Can you just set the table and put some water out?" I nodded helplessly. *Meatloaf?* This was a dish I could have eaten at my own mom's house, and in a looser shirt, too. "What about the baguette?" I asked hopefully. "Does it need some slicing?" My aunt looked at me. "We finished the baguette at lunch," she replied. "There should be some Hungry Jack biscuits in the freezer if you want them," she offered up instead.

No matter—the road is life. Kerouac was right. And in this case, meatloaf was for dinner.

Many years later, I found myself not in France, but in another country: Austria. I had tagged along on a summer trip with my brother John and his friend Joey; the two of them had graduated from college the previous May, and I had just completed my sophomore year. We started our trip in London and visited Amsterdam, Paris, Berlin, and Munich before ending up in Salzburg.

This city, which means "Salt Fortress," was also where the greatest movie on Earth was filmed: *The Sound of Music*. Accordingly, there was no shortage of bus tours offering fans the chance to visit its film locations up close. Now, I acknowledge that some readers might interpret such a bus tour as a "tourist trap" or a "fun attraction." These readers might claim that such a tour would violate my Rule #4 of Travel (Avoid Tourist Traps). However, even though the bus might be populated with tourists, I knew that *I myself was not merely a tourist*. Quite the opposite: I was a cinephile who had never felt more at home.

As previously discussed, I have loved *The Sound of Music* since the day it got stuck in my VHS recorder when I was seven. John and I used to perform the famous dining room scene in which Fräulein is late to dinner (he was the Captain; I was Fräulein Maria) at family reunions. I even once tried to make a dress out of curtains! This movie lives deep within my soul, and to say no to a bus tour featuring its most glorious moments simply because it might be considered "kitschy" would have violated my Rule #5 of Travel:

5) If you find yourself with the opportunity to go on a bus and drive around looking at statues and trees and a lake from *The Sound of Music* film set, grab it.

I decided on a Panorama Tours tour; I even convinced John and Joey to join me. I had risen early that morning to make sure that my hair was washed and my outfit was clean—we had been living out of backpacks—because a *Sound of Music* bus tour demanded the most elegant version of myself. The three of us crowded into the back of a large white van along with twelve other people, and then we were off.

And that is when everything went wrong.

"On the left, you can see Mirabell Gardens," our tour guide, Jonathan, shouted. Jonathan was from Kansas; I know this because it said so on his nametag. There was no microphone in the van, so Jonathan just yelled. He was also driving the van and couldn't turn around to face us; he just glanced at us occasionally in the rearview mirror. "This is where the song 'Sixteen Going on Seventeen' was filmed," Jonathan cried.

My jaw dropped open. Was he joking? "Sixteen Going on

Seventeen" was filmed in a gazebo in a backyard. "Do-Re-Mi" was the song filmed at Mirabell Gardens.

Should I say something? I looked helplessly at John. John was already asleep. I raised my hand. "I think—I think it was 'Do-Re-Mi,'" I said meekly. Jonathan didn't hear me. Or maybe he just didn't *want* to hear me.

I was quiet, but I was not blind.

Our next stop was Leopoldskron Lake. Anyone with even a passing familiarity of *The Sound of Music* knows that this lake is where Fräulein Maria and the kids stand up and wave to Captain von Trapp before losing their balance and falling out of a boat. Some fans consider this to be "the famous boating scene." Jonathan begged to differ.

"Here is the lake that is featured during the song 'Do-Re-Mi'!" he screamed.

I almost had to laugh. *So now you're interested in "Do-Re-Mi,"* I thought to myself. *Suddenly you can't get enough "fa-so-la-ti,"* I continued, throwing in some of the additional lyrics to that song.

"I think this is the lake where the gang falls out of the boat," I said loudly to the rider behind me (Joey was now asleep, too). The rider looked at me, confused. Then she said something in another language—but I have no way of ever knowing what language it was.

Here is the thing. This tour guide, this Jonathan from Kansas, was filling the van with false information. He couldn't get a single fact right, and he was reckless with the position of power that had been given to him. I felt that it was my obligation to right the course, to set the record straight.

And then I remembered my Sixth Rule of Travel:

6) When in Salzburg, do as the Salzburgians do.

Even though Jonathan was from Kansas, and not from Salzburg at all, I ultimately decided that all I could do was sit back and let the fake news fly.[3]

"Here's Nonnberg Abbey, where Fräulein Maria and Von Trapp got married!" "Here's Lake Wolfgang, where the famous boat scene was filmed!" "Here's the gazebo where Mother Superior sings!"

To quote the Fräulein saying her bedtime prayers for the children, "Oh, well, God bless what's-his-name." God bless you, Jonathan from Kansas!

Several years ago, my husband and I went to Japan. Neither of us had ever been, and we found a good fare on Singapore Airlines. We flew to Tokyo, and from there would travel to Takayama, Kyoto, Nara, and Koyasan. Takayama was a city recommended by all three of the travel guidebooks I consulted in planning our trip, and so we were surprised when every Japanese person we mentioned it to looked back at us curiously. "Takayama?" they would repeat, confused. "Hai, Takayama," Michael would say. *Hai* means "yes" in Japanese; "yes," "no," and "hello" were all words that we had mastered several days before our trip. I was sure our confident grasp of three words would endear us to a nation.

It wasn't until the train ride to Takayama, when we gave the train attendant our tickets, that we noticed there are different ways of pronouncing the city's name. "How many stops until

3 I should clarify. When *not* sitting in a van on a *Sound of Music* bus tour, all Americans should make a very focused and deliberate effort to distinguish fake news from real news.

Takayama?" I asked, being careful to speak very slowly and very loudly so that the attendant would feel at ease.

"You are four stops from Takayama," he replied.

I nodded and bowed slightly. "I guess we've been saying it wrong," Michael said to me as the attendant made his way up the train. "We've been putting the emphasis on the 'ya,' but he emphasized the last two syllables with equal weight." I chuckled again. I knew that I had been saying it correctly, but I noticed for the first time that Michael had been saying it wrong. "I guess so," I told him, patting his hand and smiling to myself.

Kyoto was the city where I tore my plantar fascia. This ligament connects your heel bone to your toes, and it hurts a lot when you tear it. Because I considered any time not moving to be wasted time (Ellie's Rule of Travel #3), I insisted on walking just as much as possible. "This isn't Paris," I told Michael, hustling along the narrow shoulder of a busy highway from the Kyoto train station to our ryokan. Cars whizzed by us at incredible speed, and I had to shout over the noisy engines to be heard. "You don't just sit out at the café watching the *boulevard*." I had purchased a pair of Superga sneakers for the trip; they looked, to me, to be really stylish, but they were also very rigid. Unfortunately, I hadn't broken them in beforehand, and my right foot had been aching since the moment I put them on.

Our first morning in Kyoto, I rose at dawn and laced up my sneakers for a jog along the Kamo River. The concrete banks were filled with Kyotans, both young and old, some passed out, some not, some drinking, and some vomiting. I waved and called out to these new and fun-loving friends. "Kon'nichiwa!" I cried, greeting the sun. And that's when I felt a shooting pain in my right foot. I fell to the ground, moaning in agony. An old man pointed at me and laughed. "{Something something something

something!},” he yelled. I closed my eyes. I tried to clear my mind. I reminded myself that I am strong.

USA, I said without moving my lips. *USA!* Standing back up, I embodied not only the strength of my great nation, but also its love of refined sugars. I smiled at the old man, beginning to hobble back to our ryokan. “Seize the day!” I yelled, falling again as my right ankle gave out.

From Kyoto, we traveled to Nara, which is very famous for its free-roaming deer. It is also famous for Tōdai-ji, an enormous Buddhist temple completed in the early eighth century. We had only allotted a day and a half for our stay in Nara, so I set my alarm for 6:00 a.m. the morning after we arrived; Tōdai-ji opened at seven. As it happened, Michael would not be joining me at the temple. Our hotel rate included an unlimited breakfast buffet, and it did not open until seven thirty. “Are you sure you’re okay to go alone?” he asked me. “I’m just worried I’ll get dizzy if I don’t eat.” I couldn’t have known at the time, but monitoring Michael’s blood sugar would prove to be excellent training for taking care of my future infant son. “I’ll be fine,” I told my husband, a grown-up man.

I was the only person at the gates when they opened promptly at the stroke of seven. I marveled at the grounds and the architecture. In the main hall, there is an enormous statue of Buddha; it is 49 feet tall and weighs 551 tons. “Big,” I murmured to myself.

Also housed in the main hall is “Buddha’s Nostril,” a small, square hole in the base of one of the temple’s wooden pillars. This hole is rumored to be the same size as the nostril in the nose of the great Buddha statue sitting nearby. I’m not sure why it’s just a rumor; it seems like a straightforward measurement to confirm. Anyway, if you can squeeze your body through this hole, legend has it that you will be granted enlightenment in your next life. I figured that all the great monks before me had taken on this challenge. I knew that if I didn't at least attempt to fit through this hole, my visit would have been in vain. I thought of Michael, back at the hotel, soft-boiled eggs dribbling down his chin. I couldn't help but laugh and shake my head. While he was eating free breakfast items, I was out in the world actually living life. I looked up at Buddha, a coy smile dancing upon my lips. Like me, Buddha understood everything.

There were only two other people in the main hall, and there were two security guards at the entrance. I put my purse on the ground next to the wooden pillar and took off my shoes. Then, I entered the hole. I wasn't sure whether to stretch my arms out in front of me, like I was attempting a dive, or to leave them at my sides, like a penguin. So, I did one of each; my right arm reached out ahead of me, my left arm clung to my left thigh. This was the wrong choice. I didn't have enough strength in my right arm to pull myself forward, and my left arm served no purpose but as a burden to be dragged painfully along the lacquered wood. My head was about halfway through the hole, my right arm grasping for the outside world. It occurred to me that I was not going to get any farther.

My heart began to flutter as I realized my two fellow tourists would soon be rounding the corner and would see the American woman flailing. This shame scared me more than any idea of being permanently stuck in the hole. *There is no greater punishment than shame*, I recalled from either an old Buddhist text or something my high school indoor soccer coach said once.

I coughed loudly, trying to catch the attention of the guards. If they could just get me out of here quickly, then we could resolve this whole thing in a snap. I could still hear them chatting nearby, so I coughed even louder. Still no response. "Hai!" I called out. "Kon'nichiwa!" I cursed myself for not learning "I need help," or even better "Please pull me out of this nostril."

I closed my eyes and thought of Bar Method, a core-strengthening class that I used to take back home in Los Angeles. If ever there was a time to use that core, it was now. "Embrace the shake," I said out loud, to no one. That is something that the instructors say in Bar Method when your body begins to tremble because it is tired. "Sweat is your fat crying," I whispered to the wood.

I stopped feeling sorry for myself and began to embrace the shake, or more accurately, I began to scoot backward out of the hole. This required an enormous amount of strength, a strength I didn't know I had, a strength that caused me to pass a loud rush of gas. It was hot that day, and I had chosen to wear a black cotton knee-length dress; the dress quickly scrunched up over my waist, exposing my Hot Bottoms brand pink briefs with stains dating back to 2002. Barefoot, farting, and overly exposed, I exited the hole the same way I had entered the world some thirty-five years earlier. *What goes around comes around*, I thought, wiping off my knees and straightening my Hot Bottoms. The couple had reached the pillar at that point, and I waved to them. "Nice day for a crawl," I found myself saying.

And that is exactly when I realized I had violated perhaps the greatest travel rule of all: Ellie's Rule of Travel #7.

7) Always take the free breakfast.

It turns out Michael had been right all along.

But I didn't need to let him know that. When I got back to the hotel, I vaguely described my visit to the temple, mentioning the pillar and the hole and something about enlightenment, but not going into details. Michael handed me a carrot ginger muffin that he had smuggled back from the buffet to the hotel room for me and smiled. "You should be excited for your next life!" he exclaimed.

I smiled back. "I'm excited for *this* life," is what I should have said. "This muffin tastes like fish," is what I did say.

Bridesmaid

When I found out that I had booked the part of Becca in the 2011 comedy *Bridesmaids*, I chuckled quietly to myself and shook my head. "Such wonderful news," I told my agents, trying my best to appear both surprised and humbled. "I accept the role with honour." I was careful to pronounce the *u* in "honour," and then I politely inquired after my agents' health. At the end of the conversation, I hung up the phone and smiled. *The real Oscar*, I thought as I glanced at myself in my magnifying mirror, *should go to me for the performance on that phone call.*

The truth is, I was not at all surprised to learn that I had won the role; I was born to play Becca. I had already been a bridesmaid in real life nine times, and taking my story to the silver screen seemed, to me, the most natural thing in the world. Furthermore, I was just emerging from a second season on *The Office* playing Erin Hannon, a woman marked by her naïveté, her wide-eyed optimism, and her large face. One glance at the lone scene I had been given for our *Bridesmaids* audition assured me that Becca (still don't know if she had a last name) was a creature not only in possession of, but positively *defined* by, her naïveté, her wide-eyed optimism, and her large face. I determined that I could easily tweak the nuances of my performance to portray my face in a way that was still large, but large in a different way from Erin Hannon's face, and I swore to endow Becca with the dignity she deserved. As I poured my Epsom salts into the tub that evening, it dawned on me that I was poised to make cinematic history.

There were four other bridesmaids in the movie—Wendi McLendon-Covey, Rose Byrne, Melissa McCarthy, and Kristen Wiig—and the bride would be played by Maya Rudolph. I was familiar with the work of all these women, and I was excited to teach them about comedy.

Kristen had written the movie with Annie Mumolo, and to welcome everyone to the cast, these two ladies hosted a night at Hollywood Men, a strip club near the intersection of Hollywood and Highland in Los Angeles. Having been a bridesmaid so many times before, I was no stranger to a male strip club. "Did you bring your fivers?" I murmured to Kristen Wiig, using my nickname for a five-dollar bill. Kristen laughed and told me how grossed out she felt being in this sticky nightclub. I looked at her and nodded. "You'll get used to it," I assured her, placing a fiver in a passing stripper's underpants. "I'm a waiter," he told me. "Get your hands off me!" I gave Kristen a wink. *Sometimes I mix up waiters with strippers!* I tried to convey in that wink.

Here is the thing about being a bridesmaid: it is hard. It is work. And even though the bride is obviously one of your closest friends, you can't help but to start feeling a li'l[1] cranky. I needed the plight of the Bridesmaid to come through in *Bridesmaids*, and I needed to do it with as little effort as possible since I hate doing any work after dinner.

1 I have been waiting all my life for a chance to publicly write "li'l" as it should be written, with the apostrophe between the "i" and the second "l."

As a bridesmaid in real life, I have been asked to do some pretty crazy things. I have been asked to buy plane tickets to fly to Las Vegas and Bermuda. I have been asked to purchase ugly dresses in colors that groan against my skin tone (which has been described as "alabaster," or "bright white"). I have been told to hike to peaks of hills in 100-degree weather to smile in photos where I am not happy, and I have been commanded to bustle a gown soon to be locked up in a closet for seventy-five years. And as a bridesmaid in real life, I have smiled graciously, I have bowed before my brides, and I have written back "yayayayayayayyyyyyy!!!!!!!!!" to things about which I feel anything *but* yayayayayayayyyyyyy.

Because this, Reader—this is the Plight of the Bridesmaid.

After our first official table read at the Sony lot, I began to relax. *I think this cast has something*, I mused to myself with a smile as I drove home in my charcoal Ford Fusion. *They might just have what it takes.* For the first few days, we spent time improvising scenes and getting to know one another. There were several different versions of scripts circulating, and I still wasn't sure which one we were following. I just knew I had to give Becca all of Ellie (except after approximately 5:30 p.m., which is when my energy begins to fade).

One day at lunch, I sat next to Rose Byrne at the tables outside. Rose is Australian. I was making some light chitchat about Australian accents versus British accents, and how they often sound the same to me. As I finished up asking her whether she felt more confident doing a British accent or an American accent, and if she had ever tried a Southern accent (as in, Alabama or Mississippi), Rose Byrne removed her sunglasses. I was paralyzed. *This is the most beautiful woman I have ever seen in my life*, I thought. I had seen beauty before, but never this close. And never this deep. I could not move. I could not even blink. I forgot all about the other topics I had brainstormed over the weekend to have as backup conversation (was Glenn Close scary on the set of *Damages*, does Australia have presidents or is it a monarchy, did she know I had seen only one movie in all of 2003, and it was *I Capture the Castle*) and just stared. My fork slipped out of my hands, but I was unable to pick it up. Rose asked me if I was feeling okay. I slapped my own face and said yes. Then I mumbled something about needing more water chestnuts, but ran straight past the salad bar and back to my trailer instead. I knew that I couldn't be in love with her, but I also wasn't sure that I was not in love with her. I did fifty push-ups on the floor plus two hundred jumping jacks, and only then did I feel the blood begin to flow again to my brain.

That woman is gorgeous.

I realized in that moment that I could never, ever be in a scene alone with Rose Byrne, but that was not the only production hurdle standing in my way. Now, listen carefully. I had never considered myself a Method actor before this film. In fact, I used to pride myself on my ability to keep my professional life and my personal life in two completely separate spheres. When I would finish a scene as Erin answering the phone at the Dunder Mifflin reception desk, I left both the phone and the scene at the Dunder Mifflin reception desk.[2] I do not bring my work home with me, and I do *not* invite my characters to spend the night in my head.

And yet, you will notice that I have mentioned how many times I have been a bridesmaid in real life. The more careful

2 . . . but I often stole the paper clips. C'mon, can't li'l Ellie have a li'l bit o' fun?

readers among you will see that this number is nine. But what none of you yet knows—and how could you, Reader? *For I have not yet told you*—is that one of those nine times was happening as we were filming *Bridesmaids*. Let me be perfectly clear: not only was I playing a bridesmaid in a movie, but I was also being a bridesmaid *in the real world*.

Life imitating art, you might observe. Observe again, Reader. Because it was *life that came first, in this case*. I had been asked to serve as a bridesmaid in Scott Eckert and Vanessa Baker's wedding way, way before casting of the movie *Bridesmaids* had even begun.

Art . . . imitating life? you observe, without quite as much confidence.

Yes, I tell you, grinning. *Now you are getting it.*

Production on *Bridesmaids* began on May 29, 2010. Scott and Vanessa were getting married on July 3, 2010. The thirty-six days that passed between the start of production and my friends' wedding day would prove to be some of the most trying of my life.

Now, I'm no fool. I had read a *Time* magazine article once about what happened to the actors on the set of *Apocalypse Now*. I was familiar with the risk of taking a character too far, of pushing a production to its limits. I knew that extreme moviemaking could drive a person to the brink of insanity. And I would have thought that the experiences of Dennis Hopper and Larry Fishburne *before he was yet Laurence* would be all the cautionary tale I needed. I would have thought Francis Ford Coppola's pouring in every nickel of personal wealth and still going overbudget would have taught me to remain sensible. But I learned none of those lessons. Instead, I allowed myself to sink deeper and deeper into the madness. I almost allowed myself to disappear.

I became Becca (Last Name Here).

"Ellie?" Michael called out from my kitchen one Sunday afternoon in early June, a few days after filming had begun. "I'm making tea. Do you want any?" My then-boyfriend, now-husband had come over to my apartment to hang out. It was one of those rare, overcast days in Southern California that you normally only hear about in a song. I guess the clouds and the dreariness must have reminded Michael of our old days back in gritty New York City, or maybe there had simply been a tea sale at Ralph's, but whatever the reason, he found himself alone in the kitchen with a box of Bigelow's—and he was asking if I wanted any.

"Sure, Michael!" I called back to him. I had already secured a position on the couch, cozy and warm under a faux fur throw that had come with the furnished rental. "I'd love some tea, sweetheart." I shook my head and blinked twice. I tried to speak again. "I'd love some tea, Mich—*sweetheart.*" I clucked my tongue to see if it was still working. I pinched my lips with my own hands. "Some tea would be lovely . . ." I said slowly. ". . . *sweetheart!*" The words escaped from my mouth before I had time to catch them, and I clutched my heart in horror.

What's so wrong with saying yes to some tea and calling your boyfriend "sweetheart"? you might be wondering.

Reader, I will tell you what is wrong with it. (1) I despise tea. (2) I don't call anyone "sweetheart." (3) I rarely—if ever—say "I love you." Consider that third detail a bonus, Reader—and put it in the vault for later.

Knowing me better than you did three paragraphs ago, you will now understand how completely *crazy* it was that I told my "sweetheart" I would "love some tea." That simply isn't Ellie. That's not who Ellie is—and that's not who Ellie pretends to be.

And yet it is exactly who Becca was ever meant to be.

Michael joined me on the couch, a cup of tea in each hand. "Here's some peppermint for you," he said, handing me the mug. "Oh, boy!" I exclaimed. "I love how it tastes like a candy cane!" Michael looked at me curiously. He must have known something was happening to his Ellie, but I'm not sure any of us understood just what it was. "What do you want to watch?" he asked me slowly. "Oh, Michael," I chirped. "I just popped in the original *Snow White*—the first one, the one from 1937!" Michael nodded and leaned back against a pillow. I reached for his hand to hold it, and I curled up into a tiny ball. "I love to be so cozy!" I shrieked.

"You hate holding hands," Michael pointed out. But it was too late. I was sipping a cup of tea, I was laughing at the Seven Dwarfs, and I was snuggling with my loved one.

Becca had taken over.

I knew, after that Sunday, that something was happening to me. I could feel that it was a transformation not completely under my control. I didn't know who or what to blame, either. Was it the grueling production days?[3] The demanding locations?[4] A director who wouldn't take no for an answer?[5] Maybe it was all of those things. Maybe it was none. It doesn't really matter, anyway. A reason why wouldn't change the fact that I was slowly losing my mind.

3 Usually maxing out at nine hours, but sometimes up to ten (including a meal break).

4 Mostly daytime interiors, never more than a twenty-five-minute drive from my apartment.

5 The inimitable Paul Feig—classy, kind, friend to cast and crew alike. The no he wouldn't take for an answer was to the question "Could Paul Feig come to work every single day dressed impeccably yet somehow still sensibly in a dapper three-piece suit?"

Madeline Worth, Vanessa's maid of honor, sent an email in the middle of June. "Can't wait to see you ladies in a few short weeks!" she signed off. I smiled brightly. "So excited for the big day!" I began to type. "Let me know how I can help with any details, Madeline." I stared at the screen, reviewing what I had just written. When on Earth had I learned how to use pink rose emojis? And, perhaps more alarmingly, *since when had I started offering to help people with details?*

It was true that I was excited for the wedding; I love Vanessa and Scott. Their wedding would be in New York, and I was thrilled that I would have the chance to visit my favorite city. But—and I cannot emphasize this enough—I would never, *ever* have offered to help Madeline with her event planning. That is just not something I do. In fact, I often go *out of my way* to avoid having to help with event planning. Why, I usually wonder to myself, would I want to help with tasks for which I will receive zero recognition or complimentary chocolate? No. Not for me.

But do you know who loves parties? Who adores planning? Whose passion for details and sensitivity to the needs of others is her entire *raison d'être*?!

Take a guess.[6]

"Becca" was a favorite at craft service. "Ellie, are you ever in a bad mood?" the chefs would ask, thinking they were talking to the real me, and not the character who had taken over my body. I would smile and laugh and hand them another poem with stickers and cotton candy perfume all over it. "Let's make today our best one yet!" I would cry out. The crew adored me. Even

6 (Still Becca, obviously.)

my own family began to wonder what was happening. "We love the American flag that you sewed for us for Flag Day," my dad said carefully on the phone. "How were you able to stitch such tiny smiley faces inside each star?"

My sunniness was irrepressible, and my zest for life knew no limits. One morning I bounded into the hair and makeup trailer. Melissa McCarthy was sitting in the chair, and I could tell there was something different about her. "You changed your hair!" I said, pointing to her head. "I love your hair!" The real me would have given my fellow actor the silence and the focus that we all so earnestly need before a grueling day of work. I also rarely, if ever, notice anything different about anyone. However, hairstyles and other people would be two of Becca's keenest interests.

Melissa laughed and told me it was just a wig. "It's not your real hair?" I asked. But I didn't stop there. I couldn't. "Come on—you've gotta be kidding me!" I pulled Melissa's hair, and the wig came right off. "I believe it now!" I said, turning then to sit in my own chair. Melissa's hairstylist glared at me and began to reposition the wig on Melissa's head. I smiled back, laughing. "Does anyone mind if I put on the *Cinderella* soundtrack?"

Was this how Marlon Brando felt?

I knew that I had to regain control of the situation, but I wasn't sure just how to do that. *You won't be a bridesmaid forever*, I tried to soothe myself. *After Vanessa and Scott's wedding, you will simply be playing a character*. But July 3 came and went, and still I felt like Becca. *Always a bridesmaid* . . . I thought. I couldn't remember the rest of the saying in that moment, but I found the first part to be really, really true.

I had not yet hit rock bottom, but I was so close I could smell the biotite. And then, one fateful Friday evening in Culver City, I rose again from ashes.

In the movie, there is a scene in which all the bridesmaids except beautiful Rose get food poisoning. There is a lot of puking and diarrhea. It took time to get everything just right, and we filmed many takes. My own vomit mixture was a scrumptious blend of graham crackers, vanilla pudding, and whipped cream provided to me by the prop department, and let's just say, I could have kept vomiting all night. That's how tasty it was!

During a lighting setup change, I asked Wendi how her vomit mixture tasted. Wendi's character spent more time hunched over a toilet than any of us, and I figured this would be a stimulating topic for a chat. "It's actually delicious," she told me. "Full of bananas, which I love." I started to reply, and then stopped short. *What did she just say?* I thought to myself. *Did Wendi just say she got bananas in her vomit mixture?* Now, I love bananas. I eat one with breakfast nearly every morning. So why on Earth did Wendi get to have all the fun?

Wait a minute, I quickly realized. I knocked on my head. *Who's there?* I knew that Becca would never think such a jealous thought. I knew that she would take whatever vomit mixture was provided to her and smile.

But do you know who *does* care about details like prop food? Do you know who *would* allow this omission of bananas to derail her day? Do you know who *definitely* gets competitive about who has the best snack?

Take a guess.[7]

Reader, I had returned. The real Ellie was back. And the

7 Me! It was me. I was back. (Ellie.)

character of Becca existed fiercely, but only temporarily, between "Action!" and "Cut!"

Goodbye, Becca, I whispered to myself during that night's drive home in the Fusion. *That's a wrap on Becca*, I went on. And then, like the real Ellie I was, I dared to dream a bit bigger.

And the Oscar nomination goes to . . . I thought to myself with a smile.[8]

8 Not me. Kristen Wiig and Annie Mumolo for Best Original Screenplay, and Melissa McCarthy for Best Supporting Actress.

Slob

Here are all the things my husband believes will kill you:

- cell phones
- cordless phones
- the sun on a sunny day
- the sun on a cloudy day
- the sun on a rainy day
- rain
- air-conditioning to the point where it is comfortable
- anything that has touched the floor at any point in the past thirty years
- fumes from a bus
- fumes from a car
- fumes from a van
- fumes from a chimney
- fumes from a truck
- fumes from a motorboat
- various other fumes
- all fruit that is not organic, except bananas
- all vegetables that are not organic
- red meat

- cigarette smoke
- dead batteries
- New York City tap water
- my hands after I touch my cell phone
- my hands after I eat nonorganic fruit
- my hands after I put poison on them
- the microwave
- airplanes
- mosquitos
- a spot of water or a piece of dust if either one has landed on his glasses

Here are all the things I believe will kill you:

- cigarette smoke

I am sure that most of the things my husband believes will kill you will, in fact, eventually kill you. I started looking up some of these substances to determine their toxicity and then got too depressed to keep going. Lots of these items could make you sick, but most of them have to be experienced pretty extremely to have a harmful effect. Anyway, we can't live in a bubble of sterility. I can't stop eating dead batteries just because there is a slight "risk" to my life. I have to be who I am.

Here is who I am: I am a woman who doesn't always wash her hands after going to the bathroom at home. Yes, that's sick, but how sick is it? I'm not touching anything but toilet paper when I go to the bathroom. I'm in my own home, so I have to assume the flush handle is clean enough. And I have really dry hands. Washing my hands aggravates this condition. For this reason, you can see why I try to avoid unnecessary handwashing.

Once, my husband was a witness to this. He and I were both in the bathroom; he was brushing his teeth, and I was, as the professionals say, going pee pee. I finished, flushed the toilet, and absentmindedly turned on the sink faucet for my usual five seconds. Then I turned it off without running my hands under the water. "You didn't wash your hands," he said, his mouth full of toothpaste.

"I know," I said. "They aren't dirty." My husband spat in the sink. "You just went *to the bathroom*," he told me. "But my *hands aren't dirty*," I repeated, getting louder. "I have dry hands!"

Michael was speechless for a moment. He was foaming at the mouth, and I had to remind myself that it was just toothpaste. He took a deep breath and steadied himself against the vanity. "Why did you run the water?" he asked. "Were you planning to wash your hands and then you forgot?" His eyes looked hopeful.

I looked down at the floor for a minute. Then I looked back up at him. "I didn't forget," I said quietly. "I was never going to wash them. I turn on the water so that anyone standing by the door thinks I'm washing my hands.

"That was the plan all along."

While I recognize that I'm gross, somewhere deep within me, I must also think that I'm not *that* gross. I like the outdoors—I like dirt. I don't always wash fruit, I rarely shower after a plane ride, and I'll eat Cheez-Its off the floor up to fifty minutes after they fell. I used to brag about how rarely I get sick, and then I noticed that I actually get sick quite a bit. So maybe I should sanitize a bit more. But maybe not.

I had to assume, with my laid-back approach toward germs, that I would be pretty cool if I ever had a baby. When asked,[1] I

1 Nobody ever asked me about this.

predicted that I would be the kind of relaxed mom you see at the coffeehouse, the one who gives her baby 100 percent of her attention while also casually enjoying a latté with the elderly widow from her apartment co-op. When her baby drops her bottle on the ground, this cool mom picks it up and gives it back to her. She doesn't run screaming to the barista for an antiseptic; she asks the old widow a little more about what it was like being a homemaker during World War II. She giggles a little bit, pulls out a Mason jar of overnight oats from her reusable grocery tote, feeds both herself and her baby with the same spoon, and finally leaves the coffeehouse for the subway with comfort and ease, because this mom understands that New York City Transit germs are the very best germs *in the world*.

There was just one problem with this vision, and it was one that I could not possibly have foreseen: the world is a disgusting place.

How did this happen? Where had all of these germs and danger been hiding? For the first thirty-six years of my life, I walked on this Earth unafraid and alive. I shook people's hands during the Peace Be with You section of Mass; I pressed my face right up to the microwave to watch the meat defrost. Wildlife didn't scare me, and neither did a tall bathtub. Then, in July of my thirty-sixth year, I had a baby—and everything changed.

Suddenly, floors were dirty. Sponges were deadly. A sneeze from across the apartment threatened my family's very existence. "Did you wash your hands?" I shriek, as Michael leans down to pick up our wailing newborn. "I think I did," he says, panicked. "Wait a minute. Did I?!" He puts our five-day-old baby back in the bassinet and races to the kitchen. I run after him and nearly knock him over trying to scrub my own paws. "I'm just—I'm so scared," I whisper to Michael. We hold each other close as our son, James, wails from his bassinet because he is hungry, and his mom and dad are holding each other instead of feeding him.

We don't give swaddling a minute's thought. "It's too risky," I say to Michael, as we watch James sleep. "The blanket could creep up over his face," he agrees. "It feels like this trendy new trick[2] and I'm just not convinced that it's a safe way to soothe the baby," I conclude, and we both fall asleep on the couch until James wakes up eighteen minutes later.

James has his very first visit to the pediatrician when he is only a week old. We are living in the West Village, and the doctor's office is less than a mile away. However, it is August, and we worry about the sun's rays. "I know it's only eight a.m.," I say to Michael as we pack James's bag like we are going on a months-long safari, "but it's the height of summer." Michael nods. "I don't like James being out in all that air," he says, inspecting a small spot on James's cheek. "What is this spot?!" he cries. I lean in to look. "It was some dust," I say gravely. "James had some dust on his cheek." We stare at each other and shake our heads. But we know that it is time to figure out our route to Dr. Barney Softness, MD.

We don't trust a taxi driver, and there is no subway or bus route that wouldn't require a fair amount of walking. Instead, we decide to use a service called Kid Rides. "These drivers will be both parents *and* drivers," I assume out loud. The Kid Rides car pulls up, and it is enormous. It is almost a bus, but it's not. I immediately ask the driver if she has any children. "Try four," she says, smiling. I wink at her, knowingly. *Moms and their kids*, my eyes say. She straps our car seat into the car as though she

2 Earliest depictions of swaddled babies date back to the Paleolithic era.

has done it a thousand times before—and she probably has. Both with her own kids, and for her work at Kid Rides.

"How old is he?" the driver asks. Michael starts to answer, but I cut him off. "She's talking about the baby," I murmur to him. "He's six days old," I answer. "Six days today," I specify. "How old are your kids?" I ask, trying to make her feel comfortable. "My kids are eleven, nine, five, and two," she replies. I look at her registration on the back of the driver's seat, which says her name is Angie. "And every single one of them is sick," she says, laughing as she turns onto Seventh Avenue.

I freeze. I turn to Michael. "Her kids are sick," I whisper urgently. "Her kids are sick," he whispers urgently back to me.

I immediately lower a window to let in some fresh air. Michael raises it back up again. "The fumes," he tells me. "The fumes from outside!!!" "The germs," I hiss back. "The germs from inside!!!"

"Does this little man have a summer cold?" Angie asks, turning on some jazz.

I try hard to smile. "He is just a week old," I tell her. "I don't know if you can even get a cold this early on in life."

"All sorts of kids have summer colds this time of year," Angie continues. "Just before I picked you up, I had a set of twins in here." She slows down for a jaywalker. "The Sniffle Twins," she tells me, laughing. "No, their last name was Martin, I think," she clarifies.

Just then, James spits out his pacifier. In the millisecond it takes to turn my eyes from Angie in the rearview mirror to James in the germ-filled car seat, the pacifier *drops to the floor.* "Holy mother," I murmur. "Lord have mercy." I look at Michael. He nods. We both know what to do.

This pacifier may as well now be liquid mercury; the nipple, arsenic. I wrap the sleeve of my cardigan around my hand and bend down to pick up the pacifier. Wordlessly, I throw it out of our moving vehicle. Angie hums along to the jazz as though she were somehow not, in fact, in the driver's seat of a Death Car. I spit on my hands to clean them before opening up the diaper bag on my lap. Without so much as a nudge from Michael, I produce the bottle of Purell, the pack of Antibacterial Wet Ones, a change of onesie for James, a surgical mask for Michael, a surgical mask for me, a fresh pacifier for James, a bottle of water to wash off additional moisture from the Wet Ones, a hand towel to dry off the moisture from the bottle of water, and a container of pepper spray to ward off potential assailants.

"Doctor's office, table for three," jokes Angie as we pull up to the building.

We pay her, we thank her, and we get the hell out of her Murder Van.

As we gently carry James in his car seat through the office of Dr. Softness, I catch sight of myself in a mirror. Who is looking back at me? Who is this woman, now fearful of dust, now terrified of a cough? I step closer toward the mirror. "Dr. Softness will see James in the Rhino Room—that's the third room on the left," the receptionist tells us.

"Ellie?" Michael calls out as I continue peering at my reflection. "Ellie, are you coming with James and me to the Rhino Room?" "One minute!" I shout back. "One minute," I whisper, leaning even closer to my reflection. I am so close to my reflection that I could kiss it—but I don't.

The woman looking back at me was afraid. She was afraid for her son, and of the many dangers that threatened him. She was afraid of Kid Rides; she was afraid of swaddling. But this woman, the woman looking back at me in the mirror—(me)—had one thing she wasn't afraid of.

New York City tap water.

I still drink that stuff by the gallon. "That's who I am," I say to my reflection, smiling. "That's who I am!" I cry out, running to join my husband, my baby, and Barney Softness in the Rhino Room.

Diva

One morning while filming *Bridesmaids* in 2010, I walked into my trailer and saw that the lovely ladies from our wardrobe department had laid out my dress, earrings, headband, shoes, and—last but not least—my underpants. On top of the underpants was a pretty pink card that read "Ellie Undergarment." I laughed, thinking how embarrassing it was that I, a thirty-year-old adult, had my underpants laid out for me as part of my job. One of my former classmates was writing speeches for Obama; one of his former classmates needed help dressing herself.

I like to think that I am tough and resourceful—hardiness is something I value. So, when I realized that the most challenging part of my workday might be to pretend I had bumped my knee on a coffee table, I grew despondent. "Am I not as brave and self-sufficient as my mother says I am?" I asked myself. The glance between my hairdresser and my pedicurist confirmed my suspicion. Yes, as an actor, I can be sensitive. But did my coworkers think I was a full-on *wuss*?

My disquiet only grew as I learned that the pinnacle of success in my profession—the loftiest peak I could hope to reach—was arriving to work on time. If you ask any crew member on any set what it was like working with some legendary actor or another, this is invariably one of the first things they bring up. There is little mention of craft, or skill, or excellence in faking a British accent. No, the glowing words these icons receive are always on the subject of punctuality. "Pacino? Always on time. Shows up to work five minutes early, even." "Streep? You'd better believe that broad is *never late*." I am alarmed. Years ago, I remember heaping praise on my three-year-old nephew, Brennan, when he came upstairs from the basement the moment I called for him. Even then, I thought to myself that this was probably praise more suitable for a dog than a person—even a toddler.

As both an actor and as a person, I want my coworkers to know that I can do so many more things than simply show up to work on time. I can break down cardboard boxes with a speed that is intimidating, for example. But perhaps most relevant to my argument that I am a competent and reliable adult: I have an actual baby of my own. I am fully responsible for another human being. The point is, I do not want to be underestimated.

I once heard Mike Nichols say in an interview that he wanted to make a shift from acting to directing because being an actor enabled him to behave like a baby. I know this man went on to achieve artistic heights and garner the kind of universal respect that most of us could only dream of. In spite of that, I will now set forth all the ways in which Mike Nichols is wrong—I am *much, much tougher* than any baby:

- I can run a mile in under ten minutes.
- I can run, period!
- I can also walk!
- If I don't like something that someone makes me for dinner, I smile, and I swallow it. In other words, *I don't spit it out like a baby.*

- If it starts to get late at night, but I'm not in my bed yet, I stay awake. Falling asleep in front of other people is really rude. Staying awake when you are sleepy is *really hard.* Put these two things together, and you might say that I am not only polite, but also that *I do really hard things and I don't cry about them.* Take note, babies.
- I don't squirm around and act like it is such an enormous burden to be flying on an airplane across the country. Listen up, babies: it is a gigantic privilege to be able to fly anywhere. Not only have lots of people never been up in an airplane in their entire lives, but it is nothing short of magical that we, human beings who have arms and not wings, can get up in the sky in the first place. Nonetheless, I would be lying if I said it doesn't get pretty uncomfortable being stuck up in the sky in a small capsule for six hours at a stretch. And guess what? It *is* uncomfortable. Guess what again? *I do it anyway.*
- I am an independent person. I do not rely on my mom for food, and I do not rely on my dad for letting me get away with things that my mom would never let me do.
- If there is something crazy in my stool, I don't make a big fuss about it.

By now it should be clear to anyone reading this that not only am I tough, but I am great at making lists. Still, I must remain steadfast in my mission to behave like a capable adult. Just as a chocoholic is one Dove Bar away from relapsing, I have come to fear that I, too, am one tantrum away from being known as a giant baby.

Here is the problem. Sometimes situations arise on a set that would challenge any capable adult's maturity. Several years ago,

I was filming a pilot called *Brenda Forever* in Newport Beach. I emerged from my trailer and fell over a speed bump. "No!" I cried. "I've fallen!" Kay, our intern, ran over to help me. "You know, someone should really mark that," I said, dusting gravel off my skirt. "There are older people on this set." I looked closely at Kay. "Not everyone is as young as you and I are." Kay was a high school senior, and I was thirty-three. She nodded—was that a smile she was trying to hide?—and finished brushing pieces of debris off my jacket. Then, we both looked down at the speed bump. We saw that it was, in fact, already painted neon yellow, while the rest of the parking lot was painted black. Also, there were those two green plastic men, the ones that say "Slow!" and are used to mark obstacles or to warn people to slow down. Still, I knew that falling over a brightly marked inanimate object was not my fault, but instead, the world's.

Two years later, we were in the middle of filming Season Two of *Unbreakable Kimmy Schmidt*; it was a cold winter's morning before dawn. I walked into my dressing room to change into my costume for the day, and I saw that there was no thong for me to wear under my hot-pink pants (more on those later). I knew that the only other underpants I had were the Hanes Her Way comfort briefs I was wearing at that very moment, and so I panicked. I ran into the hallway and asked if anyone had seen my good friend and set dresser, Ali. I was told that Ali was getting breakfast but would be back any minute. "Is there an emergency?" our production assistant, Sara, asked. I hesitated. Was this technically an emergency? I considered the question for two full seconds before closing my eyes and nodding gravely. "Yes," I announced. "There is an emergency." When Ali returned, I relayed the bad news. "I don't have a thong," I said softly, my chin quivering. "I need to wear a thong underneath my Jeggings so there won't be any underwear seams showing, but my thong isn't *here*." Ali looked at me curiously—was that a laugh she was trying to suppress?—and told me that she would grab a thong from the wardrobe truck. I remember thinking, *I know this might seem funny to Ali, but I am the one with the wrong underpants.* Ali found a thong for me to wear, and the Earth continued its revolution around the sun.

Mom

As an actress, I have played a wide range of characters over the years—characters ranging from ditzy and cheerful to flaky and upbeat. But this current role, a role that I began to undertake just over two years ago—a role which presents challenge, and prune juice, and Butt Paste, and Elmo—this is the role of Mom.

And it is the role of a lifetime.

Are there moments when I have to question what "Mom" might do? When I feel that I don't know her quite as closely as I should? Of course there are. That's what good art is all about: *asking the questions.* Here are the questions I ask the most when disappearing into my character of Mom:

- Why is his pooh green, again?
- I still see the lentils, fully intact, in the pooh. Did he even absorb any of the nutrients from the lentils if I still see the lentils in there, not broken down at all? And why are lentils such an enormous part of my life, anyway?
- Am I supposed to be applying to preschools? He's not even two!
- Why is he crying?
- Am I a good mom?

- Remember that brunch when your Quinoa and Lentils was basically missing the lentils?

As Mom, I don't necessarily know the answers to these questions. (Except the last one. Answer: *Yes, I do remember that.*) Therefore, I have learned simply to *pretend* that I know the answers.

"James is down to one nap a day," I announce to a friend. "He had the fourteen-month regression but now he's clocking a solid twelve hours at night and two hours in the afternoon." My friend, who does not have a baby, and does not plan to have one, nods, maybe unsure why I'm telling her this. "Baby sleep is complicated," I explain, taking another swig of Starbucks. It's a little hot, and I burn my tongue, all the while pretending it didn't happen because who would take seriously a woman who drinks boiling liquid? Tears streaming down my face, I say, "But James and I have got it down." James toddles toward me and I smile. *"We've got it down like Chinatown—don't we, little James!"* My friend says she has to take a call, but I notice I didn't hear her iPhone ring.

One sunny Saturday afternoon, I step out of my apartment with James in the stroller. We have just begun walking north on Broadway when we stop at a crosswalk and an older woman peers at him. Thinking she wants to admire James, I turn him toward her. "James, wave hello!" I say, smiling at the older woman. She looks at me and frowns. "Let me ask you something," she says. "Can that stroller seat be turned around so that it faces you?"

"It can," I reply warily, catching what I sense are the first whiffs of a rat. This older woman seems rather invested in the inner workings of my stroller; what exactly is she after? "It clicks in both forward and backward," I explain.

"Well," she says crisply, "you really should have him facing you."

I feel my throat tighten. "We're fine, thank you," I tell the older woman. "He likes to look out at all the people walking by."

The older woman takes a deep breath. "Do you know what you're depriving him of?" she asks me.

"I think we're fine," I repeat, starting to walk away.

"LANGUAGE!" she shouts after me. "The boy needs to experience LANGUAGE!!!!!"

"HE SPEAKS BOTH SPANISH AND ALSO ENGLISH!" I yell over my shoulder. That, obviously, is a lie. James says one word: "Da." But his babysitter speaks Spanish to him, and I can plainly see that he *understands everything*.

I fume as I tear up the street. I explain to James what has just happened. "Some people, James, are crazy," I tell him. "Some people think they can barge in and give you their opinion even though *you didn't ask for it*."

"Da," James replies.

We turn into Harry's Shoes for Kids and write our name down on the wait list. I am so rattled from our encounter that I write "Julian." "Some people think they know how to take care of children better than anyone else," I announce to James, who has long ago lost interest in the story and is waving hello to a flip-flop.

We buy James some new shoes, and head to Riverside Park to eat lunch. As James sits in the stroller and I sit on the bench, I practice Spanish with him. I don't know Spanish, but I do not let this get in the way of acting as though I do. "Hola, James," I say as he nibbles on a cracker. "Anciana, no está bien." This means "The old lady, she is not good," and I know this because I looked it up on Google Translate right before I opened James's lunch sack. "James, where are your orejas?" I ask as a Spanish-speaking couple walks by. I wave knowingly at the couple, in the way that only people who speak the same language can, but they do not wave back. "James," I repeat. "Orejas." I heard our babysitter say this word once, and I asked her what it meant; it means "ears." James points to his nose and I laugh uproariously. "He's joking!" I exclaim. Nobody around me seems to care.

After lunch, we return home for a nap. James cries his usual ten minutes before falling asleep, and as soon as he does, I cry my usual ten minutes and then fall asleep, too.

An hour later, I wake up, feeling unsettled and out of sorts. James is still asleep, and I walk to the kitchen for a glass of water. As I take my first sip, it hits me; the older woman with the stroller issues had visited me in my dream. And her name was Sandra. I shudder, images from the dream flooding over me.

James and I are in Central Park, floating above the Reservoir. "*Turn the stroller seat around to face you,*" Sandra whispers from behind us, extending an old, gnarled index finger and pointing at the button that releases the seat. "*Language language language!*" she cries.

Next, I am in my own childhood home, dressed up as Dorothy from *The Wizard of Oz*. As I open my suitcase where I thought I had hidden Toto, Sandra pops up. "*Did you turn it around?!*" she asks. She turns her wrinkled hand upside down, pointing her thumb to the floor. *"Thumbs-down!!! Zero thumbs-up!! And zero language for Julian!!!"*

"His name is James!" I try to shout. But my mouth is glued shut with Elmer's Glue. Which is usually barely strong enough to hold two pieces of construction paper together, let alone mothers' lips!

Then I am in a gondola in the canals of Venice (the one in Italy), and I am pregnant. A large sign reads, "Be Careful—This Gondola Is Made of Wax!" I begin to panic—the noon sun has reached its zenith and I can feel the boat softening. My OB is sitting next to me and tells me that I am fully dilated! And just then, Sandra turns around from the seat in front of me. "*I am facing out toward the action, just as you insist Julian does*," she croaks. "*But now I am turning to face you!!!*" I call out for my husband. I am going into labor! And then the gondola lifts from the waters and begins flying directly toward the sun! "But I don't have my birthing soundtrack with me!" I scream as all of my teeth fall out.

The dream sequence ends there, and I shake my head. Why had I dreamed about the old woman? Why had I gotten so flustered by her unsolicited advice? On some level, *did I think that the old woman was right?*

James wakes up then, and I go to get him out of his crib. I explain everything that I'm doing as I am doing it: "James, it is time to change your diaper. I will need to clean all the pooh from your diaper and your bumper, and then I will throw away the diaper in the Dékor diaper pail.[1] After that, I will wash my hands with soap, and then I will prepare for you a snack." I smile, knowing that James appreciates this insider information.

"Once you are older, James," I say, slicing up some banana, "you will remember your dreams when you wake up. You will tell me about the dreams, and I will try to tell you what they mean. I would imagine that at this point, you probably just dream mostly about bananas and me." James grins. "Not all the dreams will make sense," I add as I pour James a cup of whole milk. "Sometimes old ladies will appear in your dreams, and you will simply try to understand as much as you can." I put James in his high chair and he begins to eat.

"Your mom is an artist, James," I continue. "And because I

1 Do I get a free Dékor now?

am an artist, it is necessary that I continue *asking the questions*." I pretend to trip very theatrically over his toy truck, so that James will laugh at me. Instead he cries, and I realize I have forgotten to give him the cup of milk.

"But one question I'll never ask," I say, handing him the cup of milk and pretending to trip again, "is if I'm right." James laughs, and I know he thinks I am hilarious. "Because I might be an artist, James." I smile and tickle his feet as he kicks my hand away. "But I'm a mom first. And a mom is always right."

We laugh together, I pretend to trip again, and I know that this trick of mine will keep him entertained for the rest of his life. *I'm crushing this*, I think to myself.

Warrior

One Saturday, on an unusually warm morning in late September, I arrived at my SoulCycle studio in the West Village of Manhattan. "Happy Birthday!" what appeared to be a twelve-year-old girl exclaimed to me from the front desk. She held up a shiny silver bag emblazoned with the words "SoulCycle" over and over again. "This is for you!"

I told her that my birthday was in May, and that surely there was some mistake.

"Oops!" She smiled. "I must have mixed you up with someone else." She handed me the silver bag that she was holding. "This is your five hundredth ride!"

I stared at her, this young girl, her blond hair shining, her unblemished face glowing and dewy. "Five hundred rides?" I repeated. "I've ridden at SoulCycle five hundred times?"

The girl nodded a lot and asked if I needed any shoes or water. I shook my head no, dizzy from this new information.

I envisioned lying on my deathbed, surrounded by my children and grandchildren. "Mom," my oldest son, James, whispers. "Tell us again about the time you rode a stationary bike five hundred times."

I ask everyone to lean in closer so that I don't have to strain. "Son," I say. "There was a time in my life, between the ages of thirty-four and thirty-seven, when I agreed to pay money to take a bicycle-riding class in a studio lit by candles and filled with the songs of Coldplay, Pitbull, and E.S. Posthumus."

My family gasps.

"But where did you go on the bike?" asks my youngest granddaughter, a timid girl named Cabinet (no, popular girl names don't get any less weird in the future). "Where did the bike take you?" Cabinet is five years old and just learning how to ride a bike.

"Nowhere," I answer, staring at the ceiling. Cabinet has the worst seat in the deathbed room, directly behind me, and there is no way my paralyzed neck can turn to see her. "It was a stationary bike. The kind of bike that is bolted to a stand so that it doesn't go anywhere."

"What kind of stationery?" Cabinet's older sister, Morph, asks. "Was it the kind with butterflies that says 'thank you' on it?"

I laugh out loud. Morph never was too sharp. "No, Metamorphosis," I answer. "This 'stationary' is spelled with an *a*. 'Stationery,' the kind you mean, is spelled with an *e*."

"Stationary starts with *S*," Cabinet observes.

"Anyway," I continue, seriously ready to die by now, "I rode the stationary bike in a forty-five-minute class more than five hundred times."

A hush falls over the room, and I wonder why it is taking so incredibly long for Mandy, my robot maid, to bring up the Arnold Palmer I asked for an hour ago. Surely Mandy must recognize that time is of the essence?

"But why?" a child named Grand Rapids pipes up. "Why did you ride the bike so many times, Grandma?"

Sadly, Grand Rapids's question is too late, for at that very moment, my head turns to the side and my eyes close and I immediately die. And so, the question is left to bounce around the room. *Why did she ride the bike so many times? Why did she ride the bike so many times? I hope that I am the one who inherits her cool 2075 Ford Taurus. I mean, why did she ride the bike so many times?*

Why *did* I ride the SoulCycle bike more than five hundred times?

The ladies and gay men of SoulCycle are tough, but our ability to pride ourselves on being tough is tougher. The wisdom we gain from our classes is not the type of wisdom you can learn in any book. "Get comfortable with getting uncomfortable," I advise Michael, who sits on the couch reading an actual book. "Ride into the pain!" I add, heading into the kitchen for more peanuts.

At SoulCycle, they call the riders who take the 6:00 a.m. and 7:00 a.m. classes Roosters. I guess they call us that for a reason. Roosters get up at dawn—and so do we. A rooster crows—and so do I (depending on the day and whether or not I'm at work). But I would have to say the main thing I have in common with a Rooster is that we both sit on a goddamned perch and don't exactly like it when other Roosters invade our territory.

Now, you know you're a badass when you rise before the sun to take a cab four blocks to an indoor cycling class. You realize you're a beast when you can pedal really hard and really fast for forty-five minutes and end up in the exact same place you started. But you don't understand just how strong you are until your security is threatened. You don't know the fight you have within you until that fight for survival is put to the test.

And this, Reader, is the deathbed story I would like to tell my grandchildren:

One morning—knowing what I know now, it must have been somewhere around my 276th ride—I began setting up Bike 11. No sooner had I taken a quick glance to my left than I knew I was going to have a problem. This man—no, this *giant*—on Bike

10 didn't look like he had had a wash in a solid three days or so. That part didn't particularly bother me; I also hadn't had a wash in a couple of days. And it wasn't the wild hair or the mildew scent drifting my way that made me nervous. It was the gleam—the momentary, fleeting gleam—of a wedding band on his left hand coupled with the intense look of concern on his face as he spoke with Madison T. *This giant has a wife and that wife wants my bike*. It was 5:58 a.m. There were only two minutes before Rique would start to pound that beat. There wasn't *time for a change*.

And yet.

Madison T. turned to me then. "Ellie," she began. I looked at Madison T., a smile frozen on my face. The smile was my mask—my true face, the one under my mask, was frowning. "Ellie, would you be able to move to Bike 12 so we can put Travis's wife on Bike 11?"

Oh, Madison T.

I had signed up for Bike 11 on purpose. It was truly a lottery win—the pot of gold at the end of the rainbow. Bike 11 had knobs that were not too tight, but neither were they too loose. The seat did not wobble; the handlebars were firm. The fans blew on Bike 11 with breezes unknown to Bikes 12, 10, or any other bike in the studio. And yet better than any of this, higher still on the list of Bike 11's many selling points, was the perfect view enjoyed by its lucky rider. The sliver of mirror between the rider on the podium stage (yes, at SoulCycle, there are bicycles on a stage) and the riders to the side of the stage is precisely the right amount to give the rider of Bike 11 the confidence she needs. With this mirror sliver, a rider is able to see only the left part of her face and her left arm. And as any decently vain person knows, when a mirror reflects only half of you, you look really good.

I can't really remember how I got to Bike 12. If I were in a dunking booth right now, and my only hope of not getting dunked rested in an accurate account of how I moved from Bike 11 to Bike 12 that early morning at dawn, I may as well brace myself—*because there is no way I'm not about to get dunked*. What I'm trying to say is, I honestly don't remember how I got to Bike 12.

"Sure, I'll move over a bike," I heard myself saying. And I did. Because that's what a real champion does. She doesn't sit around feeling sorry for herself and her horrible bike with no mirror view whatsoever. She doesn't feel furious for the rest of the day because her entire day was busted at six that morning. She sees the spin class for what it is—a really fun and invigorating exercise class—and doesn't scream into a towel in the locker room after class about the injustice of it all.

On the walls of SoulCycle are written the following words:

Warrior

Legend

Athlete

Tribe

Pack

We Commit to Our Climbs
and Find Freedom in Our Sprints

Addicted, Obsessed

We Are a Fitness Community Raising
the Roof at Our Own Cardio Party

FIND YOUR SOUL

As I ponder these words, this wisdom, this guidance, I think I understand why I have taken hundreds of classes. It's not only because I'm a Warrior. It's not just because I'm a Legend. It goes beyond being Committed to My Climb, Finding Freedom in My Sprint, and being a member of a Fitness Community Raising the Roof at My Own Cardio Party. No, the reason goes beyond any of those things.

It's because I am an idiot.

Starlet

In 2015, I found myself in the rare position of being Tina Fey's guest at the Golden Globe Awards. This was back in the glory days when Tina Fey and Amy Poehler hosted the ceremony; the living was easy and the hosts were women. I had never attended this event before, and I was ecstatic to think that I would be in the same room as (and eating dinner with) thousands of living, breathing movies stars. Not quite thousands, you say? Well then, dozens! Like eggs in their cartons would these stars be scattered about me! I could not believe my good fortune.

However, this is not a story about good fortune, and it is not a story about eggs. This is a story about Ana.

"Who is Ana?" I hope you're wondering. Because I haven't told you, not yet, exactly who Ana is. And guess what? *I still don't know who Ana is.* Instead, like a toddler with a Rubik's Cube, I am forced to bumble and stumble and struggle in vain to solve this puzzle.

To begin, I should make it clear that I refuse to be owned by the red carpet. I hear its call. I listen to its song. But I plug my ears with beeswax and I refuse to give that island what it wants.[1] *But we want YOU!* the carpet sings out to me. *We want your long,*

1 Reference to *The Odyssey.* Not a big deal. I've read some of it.

endless legs[2] *and your daring, brave fashion.*[3] I know that a lot of women wish they had just a fraction of my ~~tendency to fart from being so nervous~~ ease on the red carpet; I understand that many fashion houses are desperate ~~to forbid me from wearing a dress with their name on it because I will irrefutably lower their cachet~~ for my face. But I value my privacy and I really am a lazy homebody at heart, so for these reasons, it fills me with happiness[4] to let other ladies rule the red carpet.

However, I am only human. There is only so much I can bear. I had spent three full days getting ready for this event. I had had multiple fittings for this gorgeous seafoam green Naeem Khan dress that was very hard to walk around in and was spectacular. I hadn't drunk any water or consumed any salt for two days. I had had my roots dyed, my teeth whitened, my nails painted, my sideburns waxed, and I had shaved both my armpits and legs. This took a lot of time, and cost a lot of money, and I was looking forward to securing a flattering image of myself on the Golden Globes red carpet.

I have worked in television for almost a decade, and I have appeared in several films. And while certain people recognize me—my parents, my husband, the frozen dairy stockers at Fairway—most people do not. Nor should they. But on a red carpet, not being recognized is just about the most privileged form of humiliation there could be. It is high school, but your classmates are George Clooney and Angelina Jolie. The cool football players are an audience of sweating, angry photographers. And the principal is Mr. Steven Goddamned Spielberg.[5]

2 Short with a definite and abrupt end at my hips.

3 Sometimes, I wear sequins.

4 rage and envy

5 For those wondering, the science teacher is Ryan Gosling and the English teacher is Laura Dern.

Back at the Golden Globes that Sunday afternoon in January, a storm was coming. (*A storm of my own anxiety*, I should clarify. Outside, it was sunny and about 75.) I could feel my palms sweating and my heart racing as I took my place in the red-carpet line. The radiant Amy Adams was currently posing on the red carpet. The gorgeous Dakota Johnson was standing just ahead of me. After her, it would be my turn. The photographers were in heaven. "Amy! Ms. Adams! Let's see the back of your dress! Let's see the front of your dress! Straight into the lens, Amy!" Amy Adams coolly obliged and worked the red carpet like the professional that she is. Dakota Johnson stepped up to bat. The photographers were beside themselves. "Dakota! Show me that smile, Dakota! Fifty shades of Dakota!" Dakota grinned at the photographers' jokes, the cameras flashed, and everyone was happy.

Then, well, it was time for me.

There were different sections of photographers, and each section was marked on the red carpet with a small black dot. This way, every section got its turn snapping an actor's picture. The in-house publicist guided me to the first of these black dots, where I planted both feet and put my right hand on my hip. I should mention here that I know three poses for the red carpet: my right hand on my hip, my left hand on my hip, and both hands on my hips. I don't like to use all of my tricks at once, however, so I had already decided that for the first dot, I would only keep my right hand on my hip. I ran my tongue over my teeth to make sure that there was no lipstick or cheese on them. And then, it was go time. I smiled coyly, not giving a lot, but agreeing to give just enough. My aim was to whet the photographers' appetite, leaving them hungry for more.

As it happened, they didn't end up hungry for more, because nothing happened. All the cameras had gone down, and anyone who did meet my gaze quickly looked away. *Go on*, I dared them. *Photograph me*. The photographers' lack of interest was strong, but my vanity was stronger. I smiled harder at them, willing them into submission. Forcing them to concede! And still, not a flash.

But then.

A stout, middle-aged woman in the front row made a sound. "Ana," she murmured. Because everyone else was silent, I was able to hear her. I assumed that either Anna Faris or Anna Kendrick was behind me; I turned around to look.

The only person behind me was Al Roker.

Al Roker isn't Ana, I thought to myself. And then another photographer cried out, "Ana!" and took a picture.

Oh my gosh, I realized. I'm *Ana*.

Now, I'm not Ana; I'm Ellie. But in that moment, I *was* Ana. And then—like a flock of geese taking flight, or Beyoncé's hair being blown by a fan—all the cameras flew up. "Ana!" they shrieked. "Ana, over here! Ana, let's see the back of that dress! Straight into the camera, Ana. Show me that smile, Ms. Ana!"

And I obliged without one ounce of coolness. I obliged with every thrilled fiber in my being. I struck poses I didn't even know I had in me—poses no one even knew existed.[6] And I was smiling with that ugly kind of smile that you use only when you're actually having fun. It was genuine, and pure, and it looked like I had eaten something that tasted bad. But I hadn't eaten anything that tasted bad; I was just happy.

I was Ana.

6 Right hand holding clutch, left hand scratching right elbow.

Burnout

Here is a doctor's note from September 2015.

History of Present Illness
Ellie Kemper is a 35 year old actor with weakness in the right hand.

On September 14 she woke up with numbness and weakness in the middle 3 fingers of the right hand, sparing the thumb and small fibers. She also had an aching pain in the right forearm. She saw a neurologist who prescribed a 6 day course of corticosteroids. Her symptoms have since improved but still has some numbness and can't flex the index finger of the right hand. There was no pain in the neck, upper back, shoulder, or elbow. The left arm and legs are unaffected, and gait is normal. Bowel and bladder functions are normal.

From the backstage wings of the Paley Center in midtown Manhattan, I could see *Lady Dame Carol Burnett* adjusting her microphone across the way.

Reader, I had been asked to interview this American icon and international legend for an evening of comedy that fateful night in September. I could not believe my good fortune. Carol Burnett is a personal hero of mine, and the fact that I had been asked to write my own questions for this interview was electrifying. This is a prize that people would enter a lottery to win. I had come up with dozens of questions, and I was looking forward to the evening with an excitement usually reserved for Graeter's ice cream.

And then I woke up two days before the interview unable to move my right hand.

What in the—I thought to myself as my toothbrush slipped through my fingers.

You've got to be—I started to think as I couldn't tie my own shoelaces.

Well this is just the—I almost screamed as I was unable to snap along to "Walking on Sunshine" on the commute to work.

We had begun filming the second season of *Unbreakable Kimmy Schmidt* several weeks earlier. Having not worked since we wrapped the first season the previous winter, I was still getting used to the longer hours. I wasn't sleeping particularly well because my usual bedtime of 8:15 was suddenly being pushed to 11:00 or even midnight, my face was irritated from all the makeup, and I was breaking out in styes every third day. Then, this invitation to interview Ms. Burnett arrived and I felt like dancing! Unfortunately, my body had other plans. Than dancing.

I had woken up with my damaged hand on Monday, and I asked production to give me a later start on Tuesday so that I could see a doctor. "I swear this isn't some 'lame' excuse to get out of work," I joked to our assistant director, Chris.

But the joke was on me.

"It looks like your hand has gone lame," Dr. Tompkins at Weill Cornell informed me several hours later. "You've got a lame hand." This was the clinical term for my condition. "I'm not really sure why," the doctor concluded. I looked at this man and I realized that I, too, could have been a doctor.

Reader, this was not the first time that I had allowed stress to take over my body and my mind. Throughout the course of my life, I have had a tendency to bolt out of the gate a tad too hard, leading to my own inevitable physical and/or mental decline before the race is yet complete. Allow me to elaborate.

When I started my new school in seventh grade, the curriculum felt intense from the start. The school day at John Burroughs was much longer than it had been at Ladue Junior High, beginning at 8:10 in the morning and stretching until 4:20 in the afternoon. I thought that I could handle it. I thought the wildness of this new school schedule could be tamed. But even though this endless day included an unheard of forty-eight minutes for lunch, I was beginning to feel the strain.

John, who was in ninth grade at Burroughs, urged me to calm down. "It's only the second week of seventh grade," he cautioned me. "You are going to burn out." I looked at John, French textbook casually propped up on his knees as he watched *Home Improvement*, and the envy surged within me. *Dit-Moi!*, read the title of his textbook. *Tell Me!,* I was finally able to translate four years later. *Yes, tell me! Why can't I be as laid-back as John?* My brother had the ability to keep things in perspective, and I did not. I wanted to ask him exactly how he maintained his sense of balance, but I had a report on *Far and Away*[1] due the next morning, and I had yet to write the first word.

The second week of seventh grade gave way to the third. After that, the weeks kept giving way until it was Thanksgiving. And then Thanksgiving gave way to the Monday after Thanksgiving. And this is when all Life Science students received an assignment to track the growth of some kind of plant. I can't remember what kind of plant it was, but that really doesn't matter here. What matters is that I had to fertilize this plant with a

1 I know I just mentioned that this new school was more challenging than my old school, but the one exception was that in my Western Civilization class, we actually watched Nicole Kidman and Tom Cruise in *Far and Away* as an assignment.

dry powder called "blood meal." The blood meal was gray, and the blood meal smelled bad. But that wasn't all. The final blow delivered by this massively stinky fertilizer was the fact that it was made from the blood of slaughterhouse animals. Try waking up to a yellow bag of slaughter powder every morning—and then try having a decent day.

I would quietly descend the stairs to the basement before the rest of my family was awake. I knew that once my siblings were up, I would never be able to get my work done; between Billy's three-year-old babbles and Carrie's daily blast of Madonna's "True Blue," my seventh-grade mornings were not exactly peaceful. I had set up my plant by a sliding glass door just outside the furnace room. Our basement wasn't actually underground, so the sun could shine through this sliding door and reach the plant and its blood meal, and I could record the growth.

Because it was the Christmas season, I would play a cassette tape of Handel's *Messiah* as I worked. I had hoped that the triumphant notes would push me forward in my task; after all, I held the holidays sacred, and though I wasn't sure I should be combining work and pleasure together in such a showy way, I figured it would help to have some sort of balm to protect me from the stress of this Life Science project. *John has Tim Allen*, I thought to myself as I grimly measured another stem. *I have* Hallelujah. But I was wrong. Not even Handel could help.

After my botanical growth stats had been recorded, I would emerge bleary-eyed from the basement and join my siblings for breakfast. The Blood Meal Project, as it would come to be known, happened to coincide with a time in my life where I ate a Sara Lee Honey Bun for breakfast just about every other day. I'm not sure if there had been a sale on honey buns, or if Sam's Club had recently entered my parents' lives, but for whatever reason, we had a ton of these microwaveable buns in our freezer—the big freezer, in the garage. But there was a problem with this Honey Bun. I could never get it to heat exactly right. If I put it in the microwave for only one minute, it was still frozen in the middle. If I put it in for two minutes, the outside ring would melt. Because I figured I could eat frozen dough more quickly than I could wait for melted dough to cool, I opted for the minute-long microwave time. One morning, as I glanced up from that day's Sally Forth strip in the Everyday section of the *St. Louis Post-Dispatch*, crunching on frozen dough, blood meal grit embedded in my fingernails, I knew that something had to change. Otherwise, *I was going to burn out.*

Later that same morning, Mr. Mayer announced to our Life Science class that our take-home projects would no longer be due before winter break. Instead, he told us, we would have until January to complete the assignment. My jaw nearly dropped to the floor. Winter break was the light at the end of the tunnel, and now Mr. Mayer threatened to stamp out that light. He threatened to take my two weeks of sleep, and rest, and nonstop *Messiah*—and force me, instead, to continue to measure the stems.

At Burroughs, there was an unofficial rule that teachers were not allowed to assign homework over the major breaks: Thanksgiving, Winter, and Spring. Prolonging the Blood Meal Project would violate this rule. So, after lunch that day, I marched straight to the office of our seventh- and eighth-grade principal, Ms. Breza. I sat down across the desk from her, and I said that we should not be allowed to work on our Life Science projects over the upcoming winter break. Ms. Breza listened closely and then leaned in to ask me a question.

"Ellie," she said. "How much work would this actually require?"

"Ms. Breza," I replied, holding her gaze. "More work than is legal."

Ms. Breza pointed out that this was not, technically, an area of legality, and I shook my head. "You are missing the point, Ms. Breza," I said, feeling energized. "It's the *principle*." I paused. "And you are the *principal*," I added, with a smile. I knew that, even though this was a serious topic, there was always time for a joke. Ms. Breza suggested that I ask Mr. Mayer why he had given an extension to us; perhaps this was meant to help us feel *less* pressure, not more.

When I did get a word with my Life Science teacher after school that day, it turned out that Ms. Breza was right. "You should definitely turn in the assignment before the break if that's easier for you!" Mr. Mayer told me. "Some of the students were worried that they wouldn't have enough time. So please do whatever you prefer."

And so I did. By turning in my Life Science project before vacation, I had not only narrowly avoided a nervous breakdown, but I had also successfully avoided purchasing additional blood meal. I vowed never again to allow my work to come so close to taking over my life.

Unfortunately—like rules, or Doritos in a sandwich—sometimes vows are made to be broken.

Years later, in 2004, I worked at a cupcake store called Crumbs. I had been living in New York for a year, and I realized that it was going to take more time to break into commercials than I had originally planned. I began my job at their Upper East Side location that July.

I was excited to work in a bakery because I have always loved baked goods and, in particular, cake. During my junior year of college, my mom baked, packaged, and mailed her signature chocolate cake with mocha icing to me for my birthday, and I still consider that day to be one of my finest on Earth. So you might understand why I was devastated to come up against an unexpected obstacle during my time at this bakery: a complete and total inability to memorize the ingredients in the two dozen or so different cupcakes of Crumbs.

Every morning, Jae, the manager of the Crumbs at Seventy-Eighth Street and Third Avenue, would drill me. "Blackout," she would say. "It's chocolate," I would answer, slowly. "It's chocolate with . . . ganache?" Jae would shake her head. "There is no ganache in the Blackout," she would tell me, sadly. "There is only chocolate drizzle." Embarrassed, I would look away, catching the eye of a fancy lady customer poised to ask for some cupcakes. The fancy lady would quickly pretend not to see me, looking instead for another Crumbs employee to take her order. And who could blame her? I knew not what was in these cupcakes.

My shift was 6:00 a.m. to 2:00 p.m., Monday through Friday. When I left for the day, I would go home to study the menu. I even made flashcards in order to quiz myself. *Good Guy*, I wrote on one side of an index card in black Sharpie. *Vanilla cake with rainbow sprinkles baked in, filled with vanilla buttercream frosting, and topped with vanilla cream cheese frosting covered with rainbow sprinkles and chocolate drizzle*, I wrote on the reverse side.

To this day, I'm not really sure what was so "good" about that "guy."

My frustration only grew, especially knowing that I was an actress whose very job description included memorization. Why was I having so much trouble with these ingredients? Did I simply love the final product too much to get bogged down in the details?

I failed to make any friends at the bake shop. I found it difficult to connect with the customers. I was allowed to eat any baked good leftover from yesterday that I wanted, sure, but even that did not make up for the stress I was experiencing. Jae was relentless. "Are you ready, Ellie?" she would say, taking out her clipboard and standing next to the display case.

After three months of working there, I gave Jae my two weeks' notice. I had just booked a commercial for Aquafina, I told her, and I had decided to devote more time to my improv shows and finding a theatrical agent. "We'll miss you, Ellie," Jae told me. But I'm sure part of her was relieved that she was now free to find an employee who could correctly remember the ingredients in her cupcakes.

In the end, it was Crumbs itself that burned out. The bake shop chain would go bankrupt in 2014, and soon after that, close entirely. *They flew too close to the sun*, I thought to myself as I read the headline in that day's *amNewYork*. *Their elaborate cupcake wings got scorched*. I felt grateful that I had escaped Crumbs just in time—but I knew that I could not keep running forever.

Back in the Weill Cornell office from the beginning of this essay, I looked down at my lame hand and sighed. I'll tell you one thing: I sure could have used a Good Guy cupcake right about then. I didn't even care—or know—what would have been in it. I just wanted sugar, was the point. I was depressed! There was neither a diagnosis nor a treatment plan for my hand in place, and I had a goddamned interview with one of the most elegant ladies in America the very next night.

I went about those two days as best as I could. I held props in my left hand. I asked Ali to tie my shoes. Luckily, I had finished typing up my questions for Ms. Burnett over the weekend, so my lame hand would not interfere with my preparation for the interview. I left work in Brooklyn on Wednesday evening and headed straight to Midtown. I was still in my Kimmy wardrobe; in my hurry, I hadn't had time to change at work. I ran into the Paley Center, found a restroom, and quickly began putting on my dress and shoes. The heels were easy because there were no straps.

But then—the dress. *There was a zipper on the dress.*

I closed my eyes. I took a deep breath. *Move*, I commanded my right fingers. *Grasp the zipper that you might fasten the dress.* But my lame fingers refused, and I began to panic.

You are going to burn out, my brain warned me.

You are stronger than the burn, my extensive SoulCycle training kicked in.

And with that, I emerged from the restroom. I asked the first person I saw—a teenage girl sipping a Coke Zero—if she wouldn't mind zipping up my dress. And, Reader? She pretended not to hear me. So then I asked the security guard standing not too far from that teenage girl if *she* wouldn't mind zipping up my dress. And, Reader? *That security guard did.*

A half hour later, Carol Burnett was giving me a thumbs-up and a big smile. I tried to return her thumbs-up, but I could not get my right fist to clench, so I focused on giving her a big smile. And then she and I walked out onto the stage together.

Kimmy

When Tina Fey and Robert Carlock first told me their idea for a new sitcom on NBC, I thought that it was a test. "It's about a woman who was kidnapped and kept in an underground bunker for fifteen years," Tina Fey said, over three salades frisées at Café Luxembourg. "And then she is rescued and starts a new life in New York." I smiled and laughed and nodded enthusiastically. "Yes!" I replied. "Yes, I love it!" And then I went home to my apartment, drew a very hot bath, and sat in it for almost an hour. *I think they must be testing me*, I finally decided. *They ran* 30 Rock *and she was Sarah Palin. They are geniuses who are trying to figure out if I am smart enough to work with them, and the way they will figure it out is if I say, Wait a minute. Is this a prank?* Satisfied with my conclusion, I began to loofah my heels.

As it turned out, Tina Fey and Robert Carlock were *not* pranking me, and they went on to create a brilliant, hilarious, dark, and simultaneously uplifting show called *Unbreakable Kimmy Schmidt*. When we shot the pilot, the show was called *Tooken*, and it is a title that I hold dear to this day. But the name *Tooken* was eventually nixed by network executives, and it became *Unbreakable Kimmy Schmidt* instead. I suppose if Kimmy ever dies offscreen, à la *Valerie / Valerie's Family / The*

Hogan Family, they could change the title back to *Tooken*. Or even *Tooken's Family*. Anyway, *Tooken* is so much fun to say.

Before ever meeting Tina or Robert, and as the ninth and final season of *The Office* drew to a close, I had worked on a pilot for NBC called *Brenda Forever*. The very funny and weird script was written by Andrew Leeds and Dave Lampson, and it costarred Ken Marino, Stephnie Weir, and Da'Vine Joy Randolph. The great David Wain (*Stella* and *Wet Hot American Summer*, nerds!!!) directed. The show interwove stories from Brenda Miller's past and present, flashing back to her as a thirteen-year-old played by Mandalynn Carson, and then to her in present day as a thirty-one-year-old played by me (even though I was almost thirty-three at the time—not a big deal, I have a young face, stop bothering me about it). I must also include here that Brenda Miller was a *symphony conductor.* This was everything. I got to wear a lady tuxedo, bright red lipstick, and when I waved my baton, *music played.* I was disappointed that the pilot did not get picked up to series, but I still feel determined to play a symphony conductor at some point in my career.

Have you ever noticed that when God closes a door, he opens a window? *Neither have I.* But I have noticed that timing and luck sometimes line up in such a way that you can catch a break. After *The Office* wrapped, and we learned that *Brenda Forever* would not be ordered to series, Michael and I kept talking about how much we loved living in New York City. I had traveled back there for a week to visit friends, and on the phone with my agent Richard Weitz one afternoon, I happened to mention my love of the city. Richard also represents Tina Fey and Robert Carlock, and—being a kick-ass agent—thought to connect three of his clients. Two days later, on a Friday, I received an email from Richard's assistant instructing me to go to the bar at the St. Regis Hotel the next evening at 7:00 p.m. to meet Tina and Robert. I gasped. Then I screamed. Then I panicked. I called Richard. "That is less than twenty-four hours away!!!" I cried. I needed at least a week to rewatch all of *30 Rock* and then *Mean Girls*. "This leaves me with absolutely no time to prepare!" Richard told me to calm down, as it was just drinks, and I didn't have to prepare anything. There was no way on Earth that I could calm down, so I simply started Netflixing the last season of *30 Rock* the minute I hung up the phone.

Because the only thing worse than having no time to prepare for a meeting with these icons would be to be late, I arrived in the vicinity of the St. Regis Hotel at five. I had two hours to kill, but I suddenly worried about accidentally bumping into either Tina or Robert—what if they were out running errands? I ducked into a nearby H&M and sat on a plush chair for more than an hour and a half. I sighed along with the bored husbands and dads and shrugged my shoulders. *What can we do?* my knowing smile said. That killed some time.

When I arrived at the St. Regis at 6:55, Robert was already there, and I quickly sat down. He was extremely polite and asked about my family and my hometown and the final season of *The Office*. Tina joined us a few minutes later, and I told her that her hair was gorgeous. Actually, what I said was, "You have great hair—really strong and thick!" That is what I said. To Elizabeth Stamatina Fey.

To my surprise, the meeting was easy and relaxed. I had told myself beforehand that I would order whatever Tina Fey ordered, so I had a giant roasted grape margarita with just a squirt of persimmon. Just kidding! We both had a glass of white wine. We mostly talked about *30 Rock* and *The Office*—both shows had ended that year—and I remember telling them about my wedding. *Why, Ellie?* At the end of the meeting, Robert hailed a cab for me, and I went downtown to join some friends for dinner. I certainly had no idea what the meeting had been about, beyond simply networking, but I felt so pleased. They were really nice.

It was a couple of months later, at Café Luxembourg, that they shared their show idea with me. They wrote the script and submitted it to the studio in mid-October 2013, and the show received a straight-to-series thirteen-episode order on Halloween! Talk about a truly spooktacular day!

We shot the pilot in New York City in March of 2014. The headline from that experience was: cold. It was so cold. It started off being freezing, but it quickly plummeted to frigid. There is a scene in Times Square where Titus (played by the brilliant Tituss Burgess) and Kimmy are singing, and we shot the whole thing in a single morning. I kept an eye on a large billboard displaying the time and temperature, and it never rose above 21 degrees. But you know what? I was in the center of Times Square filming a pilot with the inimitable Tina Fey, so—I wore mittens between takes.

This was the first time I had been the lead of a television show. Sure, I had played Bunny Sue in *Hoppin'* and Bonnie in *Anything Goes*, but this was a whole new ballgame. I had gone from buying bargain maps online at *The Office* to doing my own stunts at Marquee! (That's a nightclub in Chelsea.) New Yorkers are tough, man, and this NYC crew—most of whom had come from *30 Rock*—did not mess around. At first, I found the experience overwhelming. From tasks as straightforward as line memorization to basic etiquette like learning everyone's name to the creative demands of figuring out the character of Kimmy, this was much more work than I was used to. My jobs until that point had been:

- Eighteenth cast member of *The Office*
- Supporting character in *Bridesmaids*
- Publicist character on Sofia Coppola's *Somewhere* (one full day of work, with two-hour "European style" lunch break of pasta with cloth napkins)
- Many commercials, none of which took more than a day to shoot
- A cashier at a cupcake store
- Drove a child actor to and from the set of M. Night Shyamalan's *The Village*; sat in a large tent while he filmed
- A cashier at a frozen custard store
- Various temp jobs involving data entry and typing
- Made the pizzas at Conway School one Saturday a year

Though I considered myself a hard worker, most of my employment experience until then had consisted of waiting around and dealing with various carbohydrates. This new job would require discipline, stamina, and sustained focus from me, and—pathetic as it sounds—I wasn't sure that I was cut out to handle it.

One afternoon during the pilot, we were filming a scene where Titus emerges from the shower. (I should note here that "Titus" the character is spelled with one "s" and "Tituss" the man is spelled with two.) Kimmy is lounging in an armchair, asking who the Kardashians are. That scene was later cut—though the Kardashians remain. In any case, during a lighting setup, Tituss (the actor!) and I were waiting on set in his character's bedroom. We had probably known each other for about five days by that point. Do you ever meet someone whom you are convinced you have met before? I don't really believe in past lives, but the minute I met Tituss, I felt confident that I knew him already. We had each other's number from the start, for which we are both grateful, because if we didn't understand each other, working together would have been a challenge.

This moment of recognition was crystallized for me on the first day of shooting. Tituss suggested that we go have lunch the following weekend to celebrate the pilot. I said, "Yes! We should definitely do that!" but everything I had just said was a lie. I am a natural-born shut-in who dreads leaving the couch. Tituss thought for a moment before saying, "Actually, I hate leaving my apartment on the weekend. Let's just text on Saturday instead." What can I say? This man has my heart.

Back on set, we asked a production assistant named Greg to take a photo of us, so that one day we could show our grandkids. I am sitting on Tituss's lap, but because he is only wearing a towel, he looks like he is naked. When Greg showed us the photo, I started laughing so hard that I wet my pants. While still sitting on Tituss's lap. He remained totally unfazed, and I knew then that in Tituss I had a friend forever.

Here is the pic:

After we completed the pilot in late March, we had a long break while Tina and Robert assembled the writers' room, hired additional actors, and began writing the rest of the season. We returned to filming in August, and I was relieved to find that I felt giddy. I was excited to work. And, it was fun being in nearly every scene. Working is much more exhilarating than waiting, I quickly learned, and the scripts were insane. Jane Krakowski and Carol Kane joined the show in August, and I had to pinch myself. These are two of America's most extraordinary actresses, and I would now be working with them nearly every day. I feel honored even to be in their presence.

The biggest adjustment for me, going from *The Office* to *Unbreakable Kimmy Schmidt*, was simply the length of the workday. At *The Office*, we filmed Monday through Friday, usually beginning around 7:00 a.m. and very rarely going past 7:00 p.m. Depending on the day, actors had to arrive earlier than seven for hair and makeup, but I was usually driving home by four or five. During the final episode, there were two Saturdays *in a row* that we had to work, and the cast was bewildered. "This is madness," I remember telling Waldo. "Yeah, what a tough life you have!" his shiny plastic eyes replied.

The Office was shot "documentary style," which meant that the footage was intended to look grainy and unpolished. Most cameras were handheld, and lighting setups were relatively quick. *Kimmy* is a "single camera" show, which refers to the fact that the scene is shot from one angle at a time. Once we shoot the scene from one angle, we move the cameras and the lights to shoot it from a different angle. This results in a longer workday—but it also results in longer naps for actors in between scenes!

I get very antsy on set, and I enjoy being outside; I'm like a skittish pony, but with human legs. So despite the longer naps, this new schedule required an adjustment on my part because I was used to being home in time for *Wheel of Fortune*.

Another adjustment was getting used to the Teamsters. In LA, actors usually drive themselves to work because everyone has a car. In New York, most shows transport their actors back and forth with the help of Teamsters. (The Teamster union is a labor union dating back to 1903; the name derives from the team of oxen, horses, or mules driven by members in the old days.) Hitching a ride this way is an enormous luxury because the actor can presumably learn her lines, stare out the window, or sleep while she is driven to and from work. Because I am chatty and pony-like, I rarely feel comfortable enough to let there be silence in the van, and I usually blabber nonstop on both the ride to work and on the ride home. I guarantee you that the Teamster who is driving me would much, much prefer the silence, but unfortunately, I am unstoppable.

One morning, I tried not talking. I went into the back of the van and told my Teamster I was going to take a nap (the actor usually rides up front with the driver). I put on my headphones and closed my eyes. I felt so awkward I could not even lie still. *Somebody say something*, I thought. *Somebody make it not weird!* I lasted eight minutes before I shot up and announced that I could not sleep. "I guess they decided on a ceasefire for the Ukraine!" I cried out, helplessly. And there ended the silence.

As we filmed the first season, we did not have a definite air date from NBC. I was a little worried, but not too worried, because as an actor, I often behave like a child and leave the worrying to my bosses. Then, as the season was drawing to a close, three folks from Netflix showed up. *What in the world?* I didn't think, because I was busy calculating how much time was left before they would bring out the midmorning Caesar wraps. We completed shooting the season a few days later, and the following Monday afternoon, Tina and Robert called me to tell me that we would be streaming on Netflix. "Oh!" I said, unsure whether this was good or bad news. It turned out to be excellent news, because Netflix is an awesome place to be, and *Kimmy* was able to find its audience. Also, we had gotten picked up by Netflix when *House of Cards* and *Orange Is the New Black* were streaming their second seasons and taking the entertainment industry by storm! This felt like a very cool club to be a part of.

Filming *Kimmy* has been a profound learning experience for me. If and when future generations of performers aspiring to play young women rescued from underground bunkers ever ask me about the lessons *I* have learned while playing a young woman rescued from an underground bunker, here is what I will tell them:

1) If Kimmy Schmidt can remain hopeful, then you can too.

One of my great hobbies in life is feeling sorry for myself. Nothing makes me feel more alive than when I suspect I have been wronged. Oh, the energy! But this character, Kimmy, this young woman who was kidnapped while walking to school one morning and then held captive in an underground bunker where she was tortured repeatedly for fifteen years, *this* woman insists on looking at the bright side of things. As corny as it sounds, when I am having a bad day, I give myself a nudge. I think of Kimmy in that situation, and I get my act together. Calling on my inner Kimmy has been particularly helpful during the Trump administration.

You thought I would go the entire book without getting political—*but at last it comes out!*

That is what she said!

2) Hot-pink pants aren't for everyone.

Look. I love Kimmy's style. I love that she is bright, and vibrant, and unapologetically girlish while being a tough and rugged fighter. And I think that Tina Nigro, our genius costume designer, is unmatched in her ability to make characters come alive.

But I do not love wearing Kimmy's hot-pink pants.

I had to wear these pants for, I think, a total of a year. I was first introduced to them in March of 2014. *Hello, Pants*, I said, in the way that Carrie Bradshaw says hello to a pair of Manolos in that one scene of *Sex and the City.* I was alone in a half-trailer when I said it, out loud and to no one, but it made me laugh, sort of.

As soon as I pulled those pink pants up, I thought, *Nope*. As we all know by now, I have powerful quads with which I am well-pleased, but in these tight pink pants, my squashed quads looked like neon sausages. It was not beautiful.

I didn't know at the time that, like the Ghost of Christmas Past, these pants would return again to haunt me!

We shot the pilot in March, but then we had to reshoot some scenes the following August. Out came those pants again! I probably wore the pants in only two other episodes that first season, but because we spent about six days on each episode, it felt like much more than that. Once we wrapped the first season and found out that we would be on Netflix instead of NBC, we all flew out to Los Angeles for a promo shoot. The creatives had decided on a concept where everything is in black and white except for Kimmy, who is bright and vibrant and *wearing those pink pants!*

I think I only wore the pink pants one more time in the second season, and that was for a flashback. And then in the third season, a happy day came my way: Kimmy donates a bunch of her clothes to charity. Including the pink pants. I felt sad for them, but relieved for me.

3) Just do what Tina Fey does.

In Season Two, Tina Fey played Kimmy's therapist, Dr. Andrea Bayden. She starred in seven episodes, and I noticed something about Tina Fey during this time. She did not say one word about her hair, makeup, or wardrobe. She put on the clothes that the wardrobe department had selected for her, and she sat still while her hair and makeup team gave her touch-ups. At the end of the workday, she changed back into her personal clothes and went home. There was no adjusting or pleas for extra layers when outside in the cold. There were no whispered conversations between actress and costume designer about "not feeling comfortable" in certain pieces.

I think because Tina Fey is a writer, producer, and actress, she is able to see the big picture. She lets people do the jobs they were given, and she keeps the day moving. I would also suspect that actresses whining about clothes is something for which she has little tolerance.

Once, while we were filming the pilot, Tina Fey came into my dressing room during a scene change. "I was thinking of trying SoulCycle," she said to me. "And one of the makeup ladies said you love it. What's it like?" My eyes grew large and I couldn't talk fast enough. "It's an indoor spin class, sure," I say, giddy. "But it's really a journey of the *spirit.*" Tina Fey nods and looks interested, and twenty minutes later, we are called back to set.

Tina Fey created *30 Rock*. She was the head writer at *Saturday Night Live*. She wrote and produced an award-winning stage version of *Mean Girls* for Broadway, she is a movie star, bestselling author, too-many-times-to-count Emmy winner, and she has two young daughters plus a husband and a dog. She does not have time to chat about SoulCycle. She was being thoughtful because she knew how much I loved it.

Reporters often ask me what it is like working with Tina Fey. "What sort of advice does she give you?" they inquire. "What lessons have you learned from her?" Surprisingly, Tina Fey does not set up an advice booth à la Lucy from *Peanuts*. She shows you how a person should behave by being the person who behaves.

Anyway, see what she's doing? Do that.

As I write this, we are about to begin filming the fourth—and what will turn out to be the final—season of *Unbreakable Kimmy Schmidt*. It always feels like we are heading back to school, but a really cool school where you get to say hilarious lines that other people write for you and the hallways smell like pooh because there are no windows in any of the stage bathrooms. At the risk of sounding like an old aunt, I have marveled at how far Kimmy has come in this show. And I will miss playing her. She started off as a wide-eyed rube eating gummi sharks for dinner and has grown into a confident woman who briefly dated Daveed Diggs. Could even *he* get me tickets to *Hamilton*? No, he could not. But sometimes it's not about getting tickets for *Hamilton*.

Sometimes it's just about feeling comfortable in your own pants.[1]

1 I know I just talked about how I *didn't* feel comfortable in those pink pants. Also, the expression is "feeling comfortable in your own skin." My point is, sometimes it's about making it through those moments of discomfort until you *do* feel comfortable. Also, I really wanted to end this book on the word "pants."

Acknowledgments

I would like to thank my magnificent editor, Valerie Steiker; my fearless leader, Nan Graham; Jaya Miceli, Kate Lloyd, and all the saints at Scribner. Thank you for your unwavering enthusiasm for this book, and also for taking my photo with Doris Kearns Goodwin so now I have proof.

Andrew Eccles, Liza Coggins, Guy Bayo, and Squirrel for our cover.

Erin Malone for championing this book; Michael Lasker for guiding me and for listening; Richard Weitz, Sharon Jackson, Lisa Harrison, Doug Lucterhand, Mari Cardoos Layne, and Ken Richman for all of your help for so many years.

Rique Uresti and all of SoulCycle. I make fun of you in this book because I am obviously trying to get your attention. I adore you.

Joe Garden, Ed Herbstman, and Chris Monks for letting me write. Jenna Fischer for helping me remember all the details of the Death Bus. Scott Eckert for being my improv partner and friend for nearly two decades. Tommy Dewey for being someone Scott Eckert and I idolize.

Tina Fey, Mindy Kaling, and Dave Eggers for your support of this book. Greg Daniels, Mike Schur, and Allison Jones for *The Office*, and Robert Carlock and Tina for *Tooken*.

Carrie Kemper, Jo Sittenfeld, Aili McConnon, Shannon O'Neill, Melinda Boroson, Curtis Sittenfeld, and Carol Kane for your advice and encouragement. A special shout-out to Carrie Kemper for being the very best sister in the world.

Shana Kelly, thank you for saving my sanity and for making this book a million times better.

My extremely funny and loyal siblings: John, Billy, and Carrie (again). Thank you for always being there.

Mom and Dad. For everything.

James and Michael. James, you are a wonder. Michael, I am one lucky bride. Thank you for making me the happiest Mom and Bug on the planet. I love you.